HARCOURT
·TROPHIES·

A HARCOURT READING/LANGUAGE ARTS PROGRAM

BANNER DAYS

SENIOR AUTHORS
Isabel L. Beck ◆ Roger C. Farr ◆ Dorothy S. Strickland

AUTHORS
Alma Flor Ada ◆ Marcia Brechtel ◆ Margaret McKeown
Nancy Roser ◆ Hallie Kay Yopp

SENIOR CONSULTANT
Asa G. Hilliard III

CONSULTANTS
F. Isabel Campoy ◆ David A. Monti

Orlando   Boston   Dallas   Chicago   San Diego

Visit *The Learning Site!*

www.harcourtschool.com

Printed in the United States of America

ISBN 0-15-335590-5

2 3 4 5 6 7 8 9 10 032 10 09 08 07 06 05 04 03

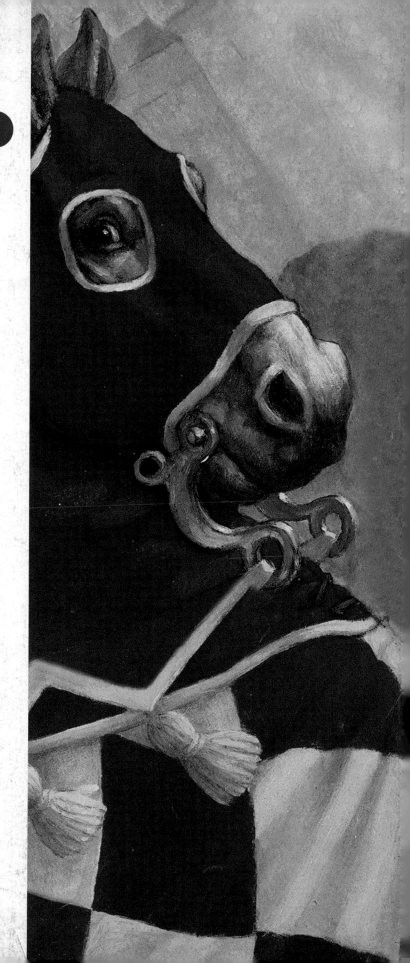

HARCOURT
· T R O P H I E S ·
A HARCOURT READING/LANGUAGE ARTS PROGRAM

B A N N E R   D A Y S

Dear Reader,

　　Did you ever want to visit a cowboy? Have you ever thought about traveling on the high seas? Have you ever had to solve a mystery?

　　In **Banner Days,** all days are great days for reading. You will read about people and story characters who use their imaginations, travel to faraway places, and work with their neighbors to solve problems.

　　There are so many things to discover. Read on!

Sincerely,

The Authors

The Authors

Reading Across Texts

Neighborhood News

CONTENTS

Reading Across Texts

Reading Across Texts

Reading Across Texts

Travel Time

CONTENTS

Using Reading Strategies

A strategy is a plan for doing something well.
You can use strategies when you read to help you understand a story better. First, **look at the title and pictures.** Then, **think about what you want to find out.** Using strategies like these can help you become a better reader.

Look at the list of strategies on page 11. You will learn how to use these strategies as you read the stories in this book. As you read, look back at the list to remind yourself of the **strategies good readers use.**

- Use Decoding/ Phonics

- Look at Word Bits and Parts

- Self-Correct

- Read Ahead

- Reread Aloud

- Make and Confirm Predictions

- Sequence Events/Summarize

- Create Mental Images

- Use Context to Confirm Meaning

- Make Inferences

Here are some ways to make sure you understand what you are reading:

✔ Copy the list of strategies onto a piece of construction paper.

✔ Fold it and use it as a bookmark as you read.

✔ After you read, talk with a classmate about the strategies you used.

Imagine That!

CONTENTS

▲ The Day Jimmy's Boa
Ate the Wash

boring

ducked

sense

suppose

tractor

Vocabulary Power

Monday

My mom went on a trip last week, so I stayed with my Aunt Lulu. I thought my visit would be **boring**, but I was wrong. It was really interesting!

On Saturday we went to a farm to pick fruit. Aunt Lulu said it made **sense** to go in the morning because the best fruits would be picked by the afternoon.

When I was putting our fruit in a basket, I heard a loud noise. I **ducked** down behind Aunt Lulu and peeked around her. The noise came from an enormous **tractor**! Its back wheels were taller than I was!

The man on the tractor was a friend of Aunt Lulu's. He gave me a long ride all over the farm. I had a great time! I **suppose** I should write a thank-you note to Aunt Lulu right away!

Vocabulary–Writing CONNECTION

Have you ever thought something would be **boring** but it turned out to be fun? Write in your journal about what you did.

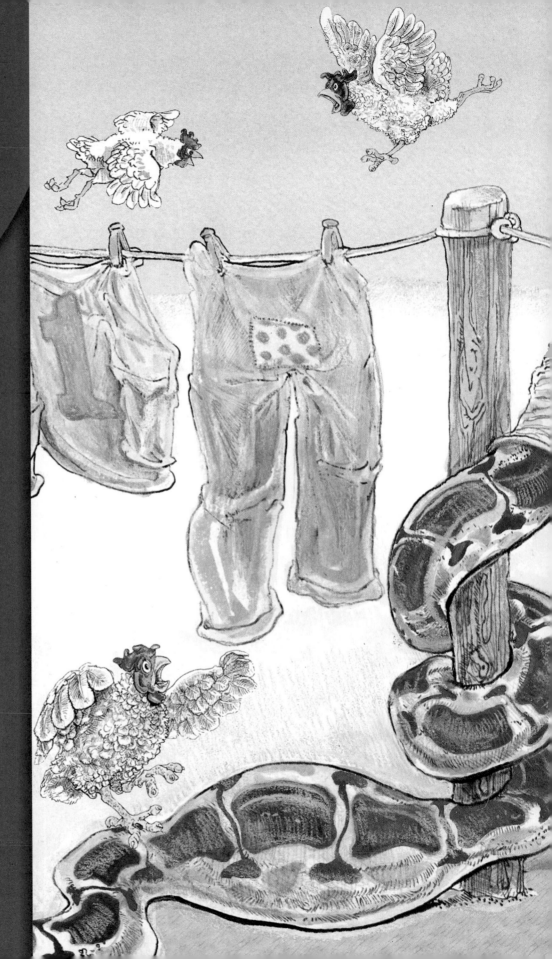

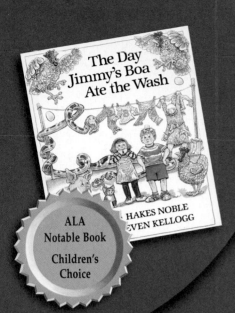

The Day
Jimmy's Boa
Ate the Wash

ALA
Notable Book

Children's
Choice

HAKES NOBLE
EVEN KELLOGG

16

The Day Jimmy's Boa Ate the Wash

by Trinka Hakes Noble   pictures by Steven Kellogg   17

"How was your class trip to the farm?"
"Oh . . . boring . . . kind of dull . . .
until the cow started crying."

"A cow . . . crying?"

"Yeah, you see, a haystack fell on her."

"But a haystack doesn't just fall over."

19

"It does if a farmer crashes into it with his tractor."

"Oh, come on, a farmer wouldn't do that."

"He would if he were too busy yelling at the pigs to get off our school bus."

"What were the pigs doing on the bus?"
"Eating our lunches."
"Why were they eating your lunches?"

"Because we threw their corn at each other, and they didn't have anything else to eat."
"Well, that makes sense, but why were you throwing corn?"

"Because we ran out of eggs."
"Out of eggs? Why were you throwing eggs?"

23

"Because of the boa constrictor."
"THE BOA CONSTRICTOR!"
"Yeah, Jimmy's pet boa constrictor."
"What was Jimmy's pet boa constrictor doing on the farm?"

"Oh, he brought it to meet all the farm
animals, but the chickens didn't like it."
"You mean he took it into the hen house?"
"Yeah, and the chickens started squawking
and flying around."
"Go on, go on. What happened?"

25

"Well, one hen got excited and laid an
egg, and it landed on Jenny's head."
"The hen?"
"No, the egg. And it broke—yucky—all
over her hair."
"What did she do?"
"She got mad because she thought Tommy
threw it, so she threw one at him."
"What did Tommy do?"
"Oh, he ducked and the egg hit Marianne
in the face.

"So she threw one at Jenny but she
missed and hit Jimmy, who dropped
his boa constrictor."

"Oh, and I know, the next thing
you knew, everyone was throwing
eggs, right?"

"Right."

"And when you ran out of eggs,
you threw the pigs' corn, right?"

"Right again."

27

"Well, what finally stopped it?"
"Well, we heard the farmer's wife screaming."
"Why was she screaming?"
"We never found out, because Mrs. Stanley
made us get on the bus, and we sort of left in
a hurry without the boa constrictor."

"I bet Jimmy was sad because he left his
pet boa constrictor."
"Oh, not really. We left in such a hurry
that one of the pigs didn't get off the bus,
so now he's got a pet pig."

"Boy, that sure sounds like an exciting trip."
"Yeah, I suppose, if you're the kind of kid
who likes class trips to the farm."

Think and Respond

1 What kinds of trouble does the class get into
on the trip to the farm?

2 How is the setting important to this story?

3 How would the story be different if the author
did not have Jimmy bring his boa to the farm?

4 Do you think a class trip to a farm would be
boring or exciting? Why?

5 How did thinking about what might happen
next help you read this story?

Meet the Author

Trinka Hakes Noble

Trinka Hakes Noble grew up on a small farm in Michigan. She went to a school that had only one room. In fact, she was the only person in her grade. Trinka Hakes Noble was an art teacher before she began writing and illustrating children's books. For "The Day Jimmy's Boa Ate the Wash," however, she wanted an illustrator with a style different from her own.

Meet the Illustrator

Steven Kellogg

Before Steven Kellogg illustrates a story, he reads the author's words carefully. He likes to picture the events in his head like a movie. Then he thinks of drawings that will show things the words don't tell. "Putting the words and pictures together is like a puzzle," he says. "That's the thing I like best about making children's books."

Visit *The Learning Site!* www.harcourtschool.com

SNAKEY

by Katy Hall and
Lisa Eisenberg

How did the boa constrictor sign his letter to the goat?

"With lots of hugs..."

In what river are you sure to find snakes?

The Hississippi!

RIDDLES

pictures by
Simms Taback

What do snakes put on their kitchen floors?

Rep-tiles!

Why did the second-grade snakes get into trouble in school?

They were always hiss-pering!

Making Connections

Compare Texts

1 Imagine That! is the title of this theme. Why do you think "The Day Jimmy's Boa Ate the Wash" is part of this theme?

2 Think about the plot of this story. Which story events could be real? Which are made-up?

3 How are the snakes in "Snakey Riddles" like Jimmy's boa constrictor?

Write a Riddle

Write a riddle about a snake. First, think of a word that has the "hiss" sound in it. That word should be the answer to your riddle. Then write a question with your "hiss" word as the answer. Share your riddle with classmates.

Writing
CONNECTION

What do you call a snake that knows about the past?

A hisstory buff.

Compare Soils

Science
CONNECTION

Farmers need to know about different kinds of soil. Gather soil from three different places. Then make a chart like this one. Talk with classmates about how the soils are alike and how they are different.

Soils	What color is it?	How does it feel?	Is it sticky or not?
SOIL 1	light brown		
SOIL 2	black		
SOIL 3			

We Need Farms

Social Studies
CONNECTION

Think about the foods and other products that people get from farms. Then work with others to make a "We Need Farms!" poster. Include words and pictures to show the many different things we get from farms and why those things are important.

37

Cause and Effect

Focus Skill

In "The Day Jimmy's Boa Ate the Wash," many strange things happen. What makes each thing happen? Read this sentence.

Jimmy was sad *because* he left his boa constrictor at the farm.

The first part of the sentence tells that Jimmy was sad. This is the **effect**. It tells what happened *because of* something else.

The second part of the sentence tells why Jimmy was sad. This is the **cause**.

Cause and effect can help you understand why story events happen and why characters act the way they do.

Cause	→	Effect
The haystack falls over.	→	The cow cries.
The farmer is busy yelling at the pigs.	→	The farmer crashes into the haystack.
	→	The pigs eat the children's lunches.

What caused the pigs to eat the children's lunches?

Visit *The Learning Site!*
www.harcourtschool.com

See *Skills* and *Activities*

38

Test Prep
Cause and Effect

Read the story. Then complete the sentences.

The Big Game

Saturday was the day of the big game. As the home team ran onto the field, dark clouds began to cover the sky. In a few minutes, raindrops began to fall. Soon everything in the stadium was soaked. The umpire canceled the game. Everyone was disappointed.

1. **The game was canceled because—**
   - ○ Suzie had her mitt
   - ○ the coach was late for the game
   - ○ the baseball stadium was open
   - ○ rain soaked everything in the stadium

Tip

Read all the answer choices carefully before you choose one.

2. **Everyone was disappointed because—**
   - ○ the game was in the stadium
   - ○ the game was canceled
   - ○ Jim was not a good baseball player
   - ○ the home team was playing

Tip

Often, the cause happens right before the effect.

Vocabulary Power

captured

imagination

manners

matador

plains

relax

vacation

I had a great **vacation** last summer at the Grand Canyon. My dad said we should **relax** after a year of hard work.

Mom asked us to behave and use our best **manners** in the car. We spent a lot of time together!

We drove across flat **plains** to get to the Grand Canyon. It was much bigger than I had pictured it in my **imagination**!

One day we went on a nature walk. We saw many different plants and animals. I **captured** a beautiful butterfly, but of course I let it go.

At a local fiesta, we saw a clown dressed as a **matador**. He was waving a red cape at a fake bull. We had a great vacation at the Grand Canyon!

Vocabulary–Writing CONNECTION

Make a list of **manners** to use when traveling with other people in a car or bus.

Genre

Fantasy

A fantasy is a story that could not really happen.

Look for

- characters who do things real people can not do.

- a setting that may be different from the real world.

42

How I Spent

My Summer Vacation

written and illustrated
by Mark Teague

When summer began, I headed out west.
My parents had told me I needed a rest.
"Your imagination," they said, "is getting too wild.
It will do you some good to relax for a while."
So they put me aboard a westbound train
to visit Aunt Fern in her house on the plains.

How I Spent
My Summer
        Vacation
By Wallace Bleff

44

But I was captured by cowboys,
a wild-looking crowd.
Their manners were rough
and their voices were loud.

"I'm trying to get to my aunt's house," I said. But they carried me off to their cow camp instead.

The Cattle Boss growled, as he told me to sit,

"We need a new cowboy. Our old cowboy quit.

We could sure use your help. So what do you say?"

I thought for a minute, then I told him, "Okay."

Then I wrote to Aunt Fern, so she'd know where I'd gone.

I said not to worry, I wouldn't be long.

Dear Aunt,
Captured by
Cowboys. Don't
Worry. See
You soon.
Love,
Wallace

Aunt Fern
P.O. Box 5
Prairie
Tumblewe

That night I was given a new set of clothes.

Soon I looked like a wrangler from my head to my toes.

But there's more to a cowboy than boots and a hat,

I found out the next day

and the day after that.

Each day I discovered
some new cowboy
tricks.
From roping
and riding

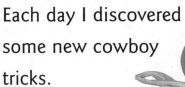

to making fire with sticks.
Slowly the word spread
all over the land:
"That wrangler 'Kid Bleff'
is a first-rate cowhand!"

The day finally came when the roundup was through.
Aunt Fern called: "Come on over. Bring your
cowboys with you."
She was cooking a barbecue that very same day.
So we cleaned up (a little) and we headed her way.

The food was delicious. There was plenty to eat.
And the band that was playing just couldn't be beat.

53

But suddenly I noticed a terrible sight.
The cattle were stirring and stamping with fright.
It's a scene I'll remember till my very last day.
"They're gonna stampede!" I heard somebody say.
Just then they came charging. They charged right at *me!*
I looked for a hiding place—a rock, or a tree.

What I found was a tablecloth spread out on the ground.
So I turned like a matador
and spun it around.
It was a new kind of cowboying, a fantastic display!
The cattle were frightened and stampeded . . . away!

Then the cowboys all cheered, "Bleff's a true buckaroo!"
They shook my hand and slapped my back,
and Aunt Fern hugged me, too.

And *that's* how I spent my summer vacation.

I can hardly wait for show-and-tell!

Think and Respond

1. How does Wallace use his **imagination** in his report?

2. What words would you use to describe Wallace? Why?

3. Why do you think the author shows the animals in the classroom at the end of the story?

4. Which part of this story do you like the best? Why?

5. Which strategies did you use to help you read this story? Why?

Meet the Author and Illustrator

Mark Teague

Visit *The Learning Site!*
www.harcourtschool.com

What does Mark Teague do during *his* summer vacations? He spends most summers—and falls, winters, and springs—writing and illustrating children's books.

Mark Teague began making children's books while working at a bookstore in New York City. The children's books in the store reminded him of how much he enjoyed writing and illustrating his own stories when he was young.

59

Caldecott
Honor

June

The sun is rich
　And gladly pays
In golden hours,
　Silver days,

And long green weeks
　That never end.
School's out. The time
　Is ours to spend.

There's Little League,
　Hopscotch, the creek,
And, after supper,
　Hide-and-seek.

The live-long light
　Is like a dream,
And freckles come
　Like flies to cream.

by John Updike
illustrated by Trina Schart Hyman

Making Connections

Compare Texts

1. Is Wallace using his imagination when he tells this story? How do you know?

2. How is Wallace like the girl telling the story in "The Day Jimmy's Boa Ate the Wash"?

3. Does "How I Spent My Summer Vacation" or does the poem "June" tell more about what you might really do on your summer vacation? Give examples.

Write a Postcard

Wallace sends Aunt Fern a postcard. Make a postcard to send to one of your classmates. On an index card, draw a place you would like to visit. On the other side of the card, tell where you are and what you are doing. Include an address.

Writing CONNECTION

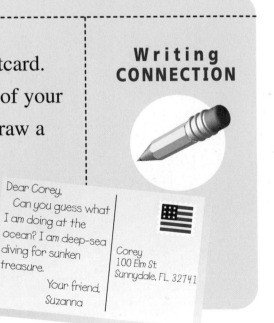

Dear Corey,
    Can you guess what I am doing at the ocean? I am deep-sea diving for sunken treasure.

        Your friend,
        Suzanna

Corey
100 Elm St.
Sunnydale, FL 32741

Home on the Range

Find out more about how cowboys and cowgirls live. Then write three interesting facts, and draw pictures to go with your facts. Share what you learn with your classmates.

Sources of Heat

"**K**id Bleff" learns to make fire with sticks. What other ways do people get heat to cook or to stay warm? Make a chart to show your ideas. Present your chart to classmates.

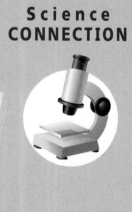

Sources of Heat

Heat for cooking	Heat for staying warm
fire	fire
	sun

Words with oi and oy

Read these sentences from the story.

But I was captured by <u>cowboys</u>, a wild-looking crowd.
Their manners were rough and their <u>voices</u> were loud.

Say the underlined words, *cowboys* and *voices*.
Listen for a sound that is the same in these words.
The letters *oi* and *oy* stand for that sound.

Now look at the two words below. What is the
same about these two words that is also the same
about *cowboys* and *voices*?

choice   **enjoy**

Here are some longer words. Use what you know
about word parts to help you read these words.

asteroid   **employed**   **disappoint**

> **Use these tips to read a longer word.**
> - Look for word parts you know.
> - Break the word into parts.
> - Say each part. Then blend the parts and say
>   the word.

Test Prep

Words with oi and oy

Find the word with the same sound as the underlined letters in the first word.

Example: t<u>oy</u>

- ● noise
- ○ sock
- ○ dog

Tip

Look at the underlined letters closely. Be sure you know the sound they make.

1. p<u>oi</u>nt

- ○ mouth
- ○ remove
- ○ joy

2. r<u>oy</u>al

- ○ voice
- ○ house
- ○ soap

Tip

Skip over choices that don't make sense.

3. ann<u>oy</u>

- ○ stay
- ○ address
- ○ choice

▲ Dear Mr. Blueberry

details

disappoint

forcibly

information

oceans

stroke

Vocabulary Power

Goldie is my pet goldfish. Before I got her, I read a lot of books to get **information** about goldfish. I wrote down **details** about how to care for her.

One of my first jobs was to feed Goldie. The lid on her food was hard to open. My father had to open it **forcibly**.

One time I tried to **stroke** Goldie. Mom said she was sorry to **disappoint** me, but this could harm a fish. I would not want to hurt Goldie!

Now I take care of Goldie all by myself. I know there are millions of fish swimming in the Earth's **oceans**, but my favorite fish is Goldie!

Vocabulary-Writing CONNECTION

What animal would you like to have as a pet? Write **details** about how you would care for it.

67

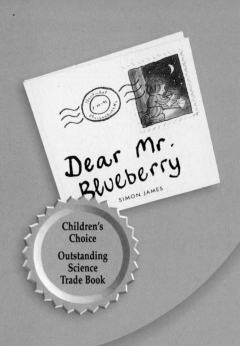

Dear Mr. Blueberry

SIMON JAMES

Children's Choice

Outstanding Science Trade Book

Genre

Informational Story

An informational story gives facts about a topic through a story plot.

Look for

- characters that tell facts.

- a plot with a beginning, a middle, and an end.

Dear Mr. Blueberry

story and pictures by SIMON JAMES

Dear Mr. Blueberry,

    I love whales very much and I think I saw one in my pond today. Please send me some information on whales, as I think he might be hurt.

Love
Emily

71

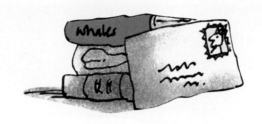

Dear Emily,

Here are some details about whales. I don't think you'll find it was a whale you saw, because whales don't live in ponds, but in salt water.

Yours sincerely
Your teacher,

Mr. Blueberry

73

Dear Mr. Blueberry,

I am now putting salt into the pond every day before breakfast and last night I saw my whale smile. I think he is feeling better.

Do you think he might be lost?

Love
Emily

Dear Emily,

Please don't put any more salt in the pond. I'm sure your parents won't be pleased.

I'm afraid there can't be a whale in your pond, because whales don't get lost, they always know where they are in the oceans.

Yours sincerely,

Mr. Blueberry

Dear Mr. Blueberry,

    Tonight I am very happy because I saw my whale jump up and spurt lots of water. He looked blue.

    Does this mean he might be a blue whale?

Love
Emily

P.S. What can I feed him with?

Dear Emily,

　Blue whales are blue and they eat tiny shrimplike creatures that live in the sea. However, I must tell you that a blue whale is much too big to live in your pond.

　Yours sincerely,

Mr. Blueberry

P.S. Perhaps it is a blue goldfish?

Dear Mr. Blueberry,

Last night I read your letter to my whale. Afterward he let me stroke his head. It was very exciting.

I secretly took him some crunched-up cornflakes and bread crumbs. This morning I looked in the pond and they were all gone!

I think I shall call him Arthur. What do you think?

Love
Emily

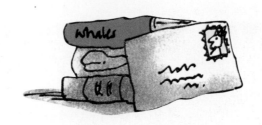

Dear Emily,

I must point out to you quite forcibly now that in no way could a whale live in your pond. You may not know that whales are migratory, which means they travel great distances each day.

I am sorry to disappoint you.

Yours sincerely,

Mr. Blueberry

Dear Mr. Blueberry,

Tonight I'm a little sad. Arthur has gone. I think your letter made sense to him and he has decided to be migratory again.

Love
Emily

Dear Emily,

Please don't be too sad. It really was impossible for a whale to live in your pond. Perhaps when you are older you would like to sail the oceans studying and protecting whales.

Yours sincerely,

Mr. Blueberry

Dear Mr. Blueberry,

It's been the happiest day!
I went to the beach and you'll
never guess, but I saw Arthur!
I called to him and he smiled.
I knew it was Arthur because
he let me stroke his head.

I gave him some of my
sandwich and then we said
good-bye.

I shouted that I loved him
very much and, I hope you
don't mind . . .

I said you loved him, too.

Love
Emily (and Arthur)

Think and Respond

1. What **information** does Emily learn about whales?

2. Who are the characters in this story? How are they alike and different?

3. How would this story be different if Emily had seen a goldfish in her pond instead of a whale?

4. Would you like to have a whale for a pet? Why or why not?

5. What strategies did you use to read this story?

Meet the Author and Illustrator
Simon James

Simon James used to be a farmer. He was also a salesperson, a restaurant manager, and a police officer. In fact, Simon James has had fourteen different jobs! Now he makes children's books and teaches at a school near his house. He likes to show children how to have fun making a mess and showing their ideas at the same time.

Visit *The Learning Site!*
www.harcourtschool.com

89

A Whale Scale

A male narwhal grows a long tusk. This tusk is really an enormous tooth!

Baby killer whales are born black with yellow markings. As they grow, their yellow spots turn white like their parents'.

Humpback whales make noises that sound like songs.

0   10   20   30   40   50   60

Length in Feet

Right whales have no teeth. They eat by swimming with their mouths wide open through large groups of tiny animals and plants.

The blue whale is bigger than the biggest dinosaur was. It can live for about 80 years.

In "Dear Mr. Blueberry," Emily finds out that a blue whale is much too big to live in her pond. Read about whales of all sizes on this "whale of a scale."

Think and Respond

How are all these kinds of whales alike?

70   80   90   100

Making Connections

Compare Texts

1 Why do you think this selection is part of the Imagine That! theme?

2 Compare Emily's whale to the boa in "The Day Jimmy's Boa Ate the Wash." What is imaginary about each animal?

3 Reread Mr. Blueberry's letters and "A Whale Scale." What facts about whales did you learn?

Write a Letter

Imagine that you have found an unusual animal living near your home. Write a friendly letter to your teacher to tell about the animal. Be sure your letter has a heading, a greeting, a body, a closing, and your signature.

Writing
CONNECTION

As Big as a Blue Whale?

Blue whales can grow to be more than 30 meters long! Go outside with your class. Use a measuring stick to find out how long 30 meters is. Then make a chart like the one below. Which things are smaller than a blue whale? Which things are bigger? What makes you think so?

Objects	Smaller than a blue whale	Bigger than a blue whale
a car	✔	
your classroom		
your school		
a very large dog		
a school bus		

Which Way to the Beach?

Find North America on a map. Then find the state where you live. Which ocean is closest to your state? With your finger, trace how you might travel to get to the ocean. Share your information with a classmate.

Make Inferences

When you **make inferences**, you use what you already know to fill in ideas that a story doesn't tell you. To make inferences, look for word and picture clues as you read.

Here are some inferences you might make when reading "Dear Mr. Blueberry." What inference might go in the last box?

Clues from the Story +	What You Know =	Inference
Mr. Blueberry knows about whales.	There are a lot of books that tell about whales.	Mr. Blueberry must have read a book about whales.
Emily tries hard to take care of Arthur.	People who have pets should take good care of them.	Emily might make a good pet owner.
Emily lives near a pond.	Whales do not live in ponds.	?

Read the paragraph. Then answer the questions.

Spilled Milk

Curtis walked into the kitchen. A milk carton was on its side, and milk was spilled on the table. Curtis's cat, Sophie, was drinking the spilled milk. Curtis quickly grabbed a sponge from the sink.

1. **It is most likely that—**
   - ○ Curtis spilled the milk
   - ○ Sophie spilled the milk
   - ○ Sophie's cat spilled the milk
   - ○ no one spilled the milk

Tip

Reread the story carefully to be sure you have the important information.

2. **What do you know about cats that helps answer the first question?**
   - ○ Cats have nine lives.
   - ○ Cats make good pets.
   - ○ Cats like to drink milk.
   - ○ Cats should not stand on tables.

Tip

Think about cats you have seen and read about.

▲ Cool Ali

Vocabulary Power

admired
fussed
haze
mimicked
notice
pale

We went to the art museum yesterday. My mom said it was a good place to escape the dusty **haze** and heat of summer.

First we **admired** some statues. We thought they were beautiful. Then we looked at paintings. My dad liked one of a man on a mountaintop. He **mimicked** the face the man made in the cold wind.

Mom's favorite painting was of the sun setting over a beach. She liked the **pale** colors of the clouds more than the bright orange of the sun. A baby in a stroller next to us must have liked the painting, too. He **fussed** when he had to leave.

My favorite painting was so small, I almost didn't **notice** it. It showed a turtle swimming in a pond. I wished I could splash with it in the cool water!

Vocabulary-Writing CONNECTION

Write about a painting, a statue, or another piece of art you have **admired**. Tell how it made you feel.

COOL ALi
written and illustrated by Nancy Poydar

98

cool

written and illustrated
by Nancy Poydar

Ali loved to draw.
She drew all the time.

One summer day, her mother said, "Ali, Ali, it's just too hot to be indoors!"

That's when Ali took her box of fat chalk outside.

It hadn't rained in weeks, so Ali drew grasses and flowers on the sidewalk. She was so busy she didn't notice other people coming out of the hot building. Some complained about the temperature. Some made newspaper fans.

The babies fussed. No one could get their mind off the heat.

Then, Ali drew a little lake
around Mrs. Frye's chair.
"My!" sighed Mrs. Frye as
she kicked off her sandals
and wiggled her toes.
"My, my!"

"Cool," piped up Ira Baker,
squinting in the sunlight.

That was when Ali drew the beach umbrella over Ira's head. "Cool!" he said again.

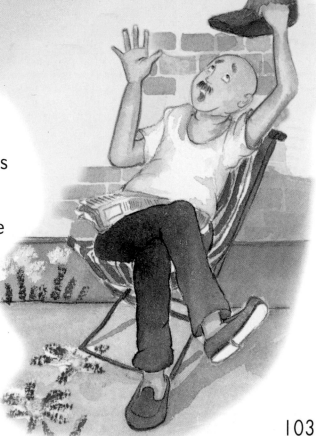

Mr. Boyle put down his newspaper fan and looked around to see what was so cool on such a hot day.

There was no more room in the lake or under the beach umbrella.

Mr. Boyle looked into the hot haze and complained, "Not even a breeze, not even a breeze."

That was when Ali drew the North Wind.
Mr. Boyle's teeth began to chatter. "Brrr," he said.
"Brrr," mimicked the babies. "Brrr, brrr!"
Ali drew a polar bear with pale yellow fur.
"Grrr," he seemed to say. "Grrr, grrr!"
"Wheee," squealed the babies as they took
turns riding on his back. "Wheee!"

"What a day," said Ali's mother, finally coming out of the hot building. "What a day!" she said when she saw what Ali had done! Then, she tested the water, admired the beach umbrella, bowed before the North Wind, and stayed out of the polar bear's way.

"Ali, soon you'll have everything covered!" she cried.

That was when Ali got the coolest idea of all.

She began by drawing little snow dots on the wall and the sidewalk, little snow dots around the big feet and little feet . . .

. . . little snow dots all over the lake and the beach umbrella. She drew polar bear paw prints and icicles, too.

She drew and she drew and she drew.

106

"My, my!" sighed Mrs. Frye.
"Cool!" said Ira Baker.

"Brrr!" chattered Mr. Boyle.
"Wheee!" squealed the babies.
"OOOO!" said the gathering crowd,
thrilled to be chilled to the bone!

No wonder no one noticed a little breeze rippling the haze and turning the leaves inside out. No wonder no one noticed the darkening sky or the first big drops of cold rain.

No one noticed until it pinged on the porches, drummed on the mailbox at the curb, and hissed off the hot sidewalk.

Then, it poured. Mrs. Frye did a jig with Mr. Boyle. The babies opened their mouths to catch the rain, and Ira Baker splashed in the first puddles that formed.

Only Ali noticed the sidewalk pictures blotch,
dribble, and stream brightly into the rushing gutter.

Raging blizzard, polar bear, North Wind, beach
umbrella, and little lake all washed away.

"Oh, no," Ali moaned. "Oh, no!"

But the crowd noticed Ali, whose drawing beat
the heat.

They clapped, they cheered, and they lifted her onto the tallest shoulders.

"Ali, Ali!" they chanted.

Ali loved to draw. She drew all the time.
Sometimes it was just too wet to draw outdoors.

Think and Respond

1 How does Ali's imagination help her neighbors
beat the **haze** and heat?

2 How might the story have been different if the
setting were in winter instead of summer?

3 What do you think Ali might do if it rains for a
long time?

4 What would you have drawn to make the
neighbors feel cool? Why?

5 How did picturing the story in your mind help
you understand what you read?

Meet the Author and Illustrator
Nancy Poydar

When she is not illustrating her own stories, Nancy Poydar likes to illustrate the stories of other well-known children's authors. She illustrated *The Adventures of Sugar and Junior*, by Angela Shelf Medearis.

Before she began making children's books, Nancy Poydar was a teacher. She lives in Massachusetts with her husband, her cat, Sunny, and her dog, Coco.

Nancy Poydar

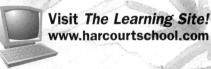

Visit *The Learning Site!*
www.harcourtschool.com

113

Cool It!

by Lynn O'Donnell

Take This HOT Animal Quiz

When things heat up, these animals know how to cool down! Like humans, animals need to maintain a stable body temperature. If they overheat, their bodies might shut down.

We've listed three possible ways each of these animals keeps cool in the summer. Only one of the answers is true. Can you guess the right answer for each animal?

The answers are on page 117.

1. Rabbits

A. take cold showers.
B. eat lots of lettuce.
C. let outside air cool blood flowing through their ears.

2. Bees

A. drink iced tea.
B. produce less honey.
C. collect water and pour it over their honeycombs.

3. Dogs

A. bark a lot.
B. shed their top coats.
C. pant.

4. Prairie Dogs

A. curl up in underground burrows.

B. stand under large mammals to shade themselves.

C. wear grass hats.

5. Birds

A. open their beaks and flutter their throats.

B. flap their wings wildly.

C. fly above the clouds.

6. Roadrunners

A. go to a spa.

B. sit still.

C. hang out on cactus branches.

7. Ground Squirrels

A. sleep during the day.

B. shade their bodies with their tails.

C. fan themselves with big oak leaves.

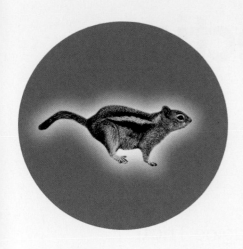

8. Pigs

A. eat ice cream.

B. roll around in mud.

C. lose weight.

Think And Respond

How are the ways animals keep cool the same as ways humans do?

Hot Animal Quiz Answers

1. C
2. C. The water prevents the beeswax from melting.
3. C. Panting makes air flow over the dog's wet mouth and tongue, whisking away moisture and body heat.
4. A. It's cooler underground!
5. A
6. C. Roadrunners hang out on cactus branches when the sand gets too hot to walk on.
7. B
8. B. Rolling around in mud keeps moisture in a pig's skin.

Making Connections

Compare Texts

1 Why is "Cool Ali" part of the Imagine That! theme?

2 Compare Ali to Emily from "Dear Mr. Blueberry." How are the girls alike? How are they different?

3 How is the quiz "Cool It!" different from the story "Cool Ali"? What purposes did the authors have for writing these selections?

Write a Paragraph

Ali is special. She draws pictures that make people feel cooler. You are special, too. No one can do things the way you do. Write a paragraph that tells the ways you are special. Use a web to plan your paragraph.

Writing CONNECTION

Why I Am Special

I make my baby sister laugh.

What's the Temperature?

Ali and her neighbors felt the heat in the air. They could have used a thermometer to measure how hot it was. Measure the temperature outside each day for one week. Write down all the temperatures. Compare them to those in the newspaper or on the TV news.

Science CONNECTION

Monday	Tuesday	Wednesday	Thursday	Friday	Saturday	Sunday

Big Cities and Small Towns

Ali lives in a city. How are big cities different from small towns? Find out about the biggest cities in your state. Then find out about some small towns. Make a chart to show how they are different.

Social Studies
CONNECTION

Big Cities	Small Towns
• have many elementary schools	• have one elementary school

▲ Cool Ali

Antonyms

Antonyms are words with opposite meanings. Look at the chart below. It shows some words from "Cool Ali" and their antonyms.

Words from "Cool Ali"	Antonyms
fat	skinny
hot	cold
little	big
North	South

Now look at these words. Give an antonym for each one.

wet	**good**
summer	**heavy**
tall	**soft**
first	**large**

Visit *The Learning Site!*
www.harcourtschool.com

See *Skills* and *Activities*

120

Test Prep

Antonyms

Read the story. Then complete the sentences.

Alexa's Room

Alexa heard her mom's footsteps on the stairs. Her mom was home from work. Alexa knew she was in trouble. She should have cleaned up her room, but she forgot. She had spent all afternoon drawing. Her mom was going to be angry.

1. **An antonym for forgot is—**
   ○ lost
   ○ worked
   ○ thought
   ○ remembered

Tip

Remember that when you are looking for antonyms, you must find words with opposite meanings.

2. **An antonym for angry is—**
   ○ pleased
   ○ mad
   ○ silly
   ○ afraid

Tip

When looking for an antonym, do not choose words that mean the same as the question word.

Vocabulary Power

▲ The Emperor's Egg

| flippers |
| hatch |
| horizon |
| miserable |
| slippery |
| waddled |

The Fillmore Times

Sunday, August 11, 2002   50 cents

New Baby Joins Penguin Family

Yesterday, a baby penguin was born at Fillmore Zoo. Zookeeper John Gordon said, "I knew the chick was about to **hatch** when I saw a crack in the egg. The other penguins **waddled** over to watch."

The chick came out just as the sun was

setting on the **horizon**. That's why the workers at the zoo decided to name her "Sunny."

Many people came to see Sunny. "I rushed over as soon as I heard," said visitor Lila Lewis. "I had to see a penguin chick take its first steps on the **slippery** ice."

Seven-year-old Kenny Stuart also came to see Sunny. "Waiting in line for two hours was **miserable**," he said. "Then I saw Sunny's tiny beak and long **flippers**. The wait was worth it. She is so cute!"

Vocabulary–Writing CONNECTION

Imagine that you are watching a baby penguin **hatch**. Write about your thoughts and feelings.

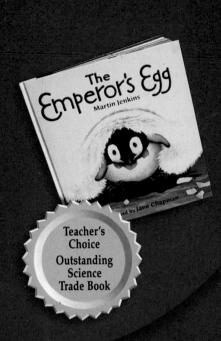

Genre

Nonfiction: Informational Book

An informational book gives facts about a topic.

Look for

- **information that helps you learn more about our world.**

- **captions that give more information about the pictures.**

The Emperor's Egg

written by Martin Jenkins

illustrated by Jane Chapman

Down at the very bottom of the world, there's a huge island that's almost completely covered in snow and ice. It's called Antarctica, and it's the coldest, windiest place on Earth.

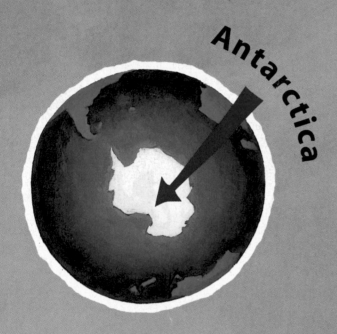

Antarctica

The weather's bad enough there in summer, but in winter it's really terrible. It's hard to imagine anything actually living there.

But wait …
what's that shape over there?
It can't be.

Yes!

It's a **penguin!**

It's not just any old penguin either. It's a male Emperor penguin (the biggest penguin in the world), and he's doing a Very Important Job.

He's taking care of his egg.

He didn't lay it himself, of course.

Male Emperor penguins are about 4 feet tall.

The females are a little smaller.

His mate did that
a few weeks ago.

But very soon
afterward
she turned around
and waddled off
to the sea.

That's where female Emperor penguins
spend most of the winter — swimming about,
getting as fat as they can,
eating as much as they can,
and generally having a very nice time
(as far as you can tell)!

Emperor penguins eat mainly fish, squid and tiny shrimplike animals called krill.

Which leaves the father penguin stuck on the ice with his egg.

Now, the most important thing about egg-sitting is to stop your egg from getting cold.

That means it has to be kept off the ice and out of the wind.

And what better way to do that than to rest it on your feet and tuck it right up under your tummy?

Which is just what the father penguin does.

Inside the egg, a penguin chick is starting to grow.
If the egg gets cold, the chick will die.

And that's how he'll stay for two whole months, until his egg is ready to hatch.

Can you imagine it?
Standing around in the freezing cold
with an egg on your feet
for **two whole** months?

*Female Emperor penguins lay one egg in May or June,
which is the beginning of winter in Antarctica.*

What's more, there's nothing for
the father penguin to eat on land.

And because he's egg-sitting,
he can't go off to the sea to feed.

So that means two whole
months with an egg on your feet **and no dinner!**

Or breakfast   or lunch   or snacks.

I don't know about you
but I'd be **very, very** miserable.

Luckily, the penguins don't seem to mind too much. They have thick feathers and lots of fat under their skin to help keep them warm.

And when it gets really cold and windy, they all snuggle up together and shuffle over the ice in a great big huddle.

Most of the time, the huddle trundles along very, very slowly.

But **sometimes,**

when the penguins get to a particularly slippery slope ...

they slide down it on their tummies,
pushing themselves along
with their flippers,
always remembering
to take care of their egg —
and trying hard not to bump into each other.

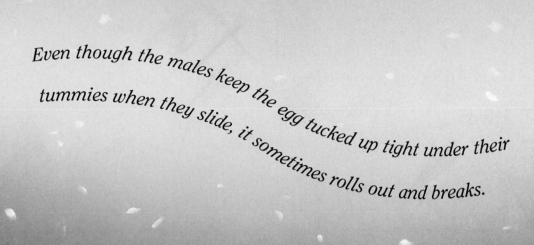

Even though the males keep the egg tucked up tight under their tummies when they slide, it sometimes rolls out and breaks.

And that's how the father penguin spends the winter.

Until one day he hears a chip, chip, chip.

His egg is starting to hatch.
It takes a day or so, but finally the egg
cracks right open —

and out pops a penguin chick.

Now the father penguin
has two jobs to do.
He has to keep
the chick warm

and he has to feed it.

*The chick is only about 6 inches tall at first,
and much too small to keep warm by itself.*

But on what? The chick is too small to be taken off to the sea to catch food, and it can't be left behind on the ice.

Well, deep down in the father penguin's throat, there's a pouch where he makes something a little like milk. And that's what he feeds to his hungry chick.

The father penguin can make only enough of the
milky stuff to feed his chick for a couple of weeks.
But just as he's about to run out,
a dot appears on the horizon.

It gets closer

and closer

and yes!

It's mom!

She starts trumpeting **"hello"** and the father penguin starts trumpeting **"hello"** and the chick whistles.

The racket goes on for hours, and it really does sound as if they're extremely pleased to see each other.

Every adult penguin has its own special call, like a fingerprint. Chicks have their own special whistle, too.

As soon as things have calmed down, the mother penguin is sick — right into her chick's mouth!

Yuk,

you may think.

Yum,

thinks the chick,

and gobbles it all down.

It's the mother's turn to take care of the chick now, while the father sets off to the sea for a well-earned meal of his own.

About time, too!

Think and Respond

1 How do Emperor penguin fathers take care of their eggs before they **hatch**?

2 What kind of information does the author give in the captions?

3 How are Emperor penguin parents the same as human parents?

4 What did you learn about Emperor penguins that you did not know before?

5 Which strategies did you use to read this selection?

Meet the Author and Illustrator

Martin Jenkins

Martin Jenkins is a scientist who studies plants and animals. He admires the way Emperor penguin dads take care of their eggs because he doesn't like cold weather himself.

Jane Chapman

Jane Chapman always paints in her kitchen, where she can look out at her garden. She was happy to paint pictures of penguins. She had wanted to ever since she saw a penguin at the zoo.

Visit *The Learning Site!*
www.harcourtschool.com

Making Connections

Compare Texts

1. Why do you think this selection is part of the Imagine That! theme?

2. Think about the problem Ali and her neighbors had in "Cool Ali." Explain why they might enjoy a visit to where the Emperor penguins live.

3. How is "The Emperor's Egg" different from the other stories in this theme?

Thanks, Dad

Write a paragraph to explain how the male Emperor penguin takes care of his chick. Use a web to plan your writing.

Writing CONNECTION

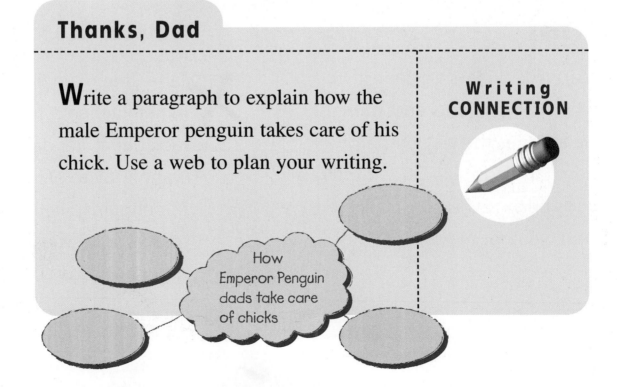

How Emperor Penguin dads take care of chicks

Going South

On a world map or globe, find where you live. Then find Antarctica. Name the areas of land and water you might travel over in a plane to get from where you live to Antarctica.

North America

Antarctica

Penguin Time

The male Emperor penguin takes care of an egg for about two months before it hatches. Use what you know about time to tell

- the number of weeks in two months.
- the number of days in two months.

Share your answers with classmates.

Suffixes: -*ing* and -*ly*

Phonics Skill

When you add -*ing* or -*ly* to a word, you add to the meaning of the word.

Word	+	Suffix	=	New Word
start	+	*ing*	=	starting
slow	+	*ly*	=	slowly

The chick is <u>starting</u> to walk.

The penguin waddled <u>slowly</u>.

Sometimes there are special rules to follow when you add -*ing*.

- To add -*ing* to a word that has a silent *e* at the end, drop the silent *e*.

  tak~~e~~ + ing = taking

- To add -*ing* to a word that ends in a vowel and a consonant, double the last letter.

  swim + m + ing = swimming

Use these tips to read a longer word.
- Look for word parts you know.
- Break the word into parts.
- Say each part. Then blend the parts and say the word.

Test Prep

Suffixes: *-ing* and *-ly*

Fill in the bubble next to the word with *-ing* or *-ly* correctly added.

Example: **get**

- ○ geting
- ● getting
- ○ geeting

Tip

Look at how each word is spelled. Think about the rules before you choose.

1.   **particular**

- ○ particularely
- ○ particularly
- ○ particularlly

2.   **freeze**

- ○ freezing
- ○ freezeing
- ○ freezzing

3.   **stand**

- ○ standding
- ○ standeing
- ○ standing

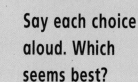

Tip

Say each choice aloud. Which seems best?

Neighborhood News

CONTENTS

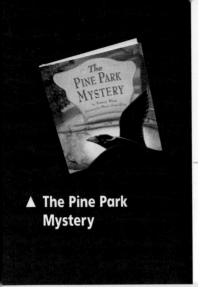

▲ The Pine Park Mystery

caused

clasp

confused

cornered

objects

removes

typical

Vocabulary Power

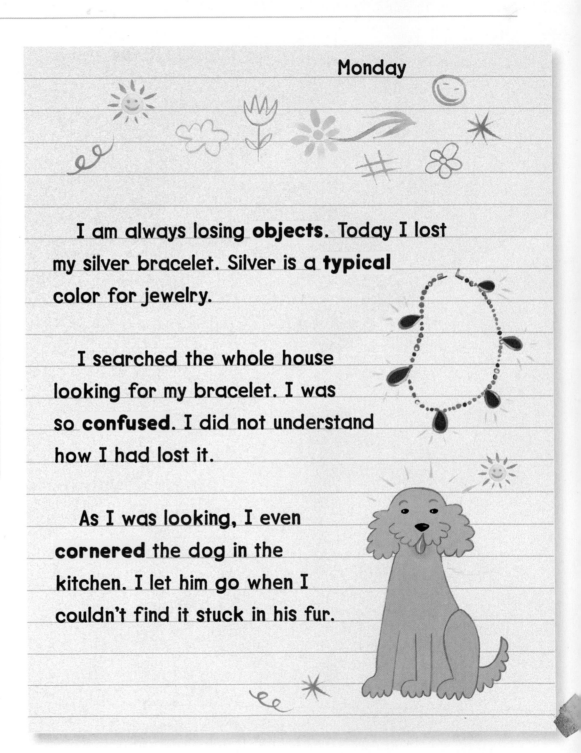

Monday

I am always losing **objects**. Today I lost my silver bracelet. Silver is a **typical** color for jewelry.

I searched the whole house looking for my bracelet. I was so **confused**. I did not understand how I had lost it.

As I was looking, I even **cornered** the dog in the kitchen. I let him go when I couldn't find it stuck in his fur.

Finally, I saw something shiny by my bed. It was my bracelet! The **clasp** had broken that held it closed. This had **caused** it to fall off while I was sleeping.

My mother always **removes** her jewelry before she goes to bed. From now on, I think I'll do that, too.

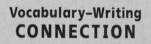

Vocabulary-Writing CONNECTION

Write about an **object** you once lost. Tell how you tried to find it.

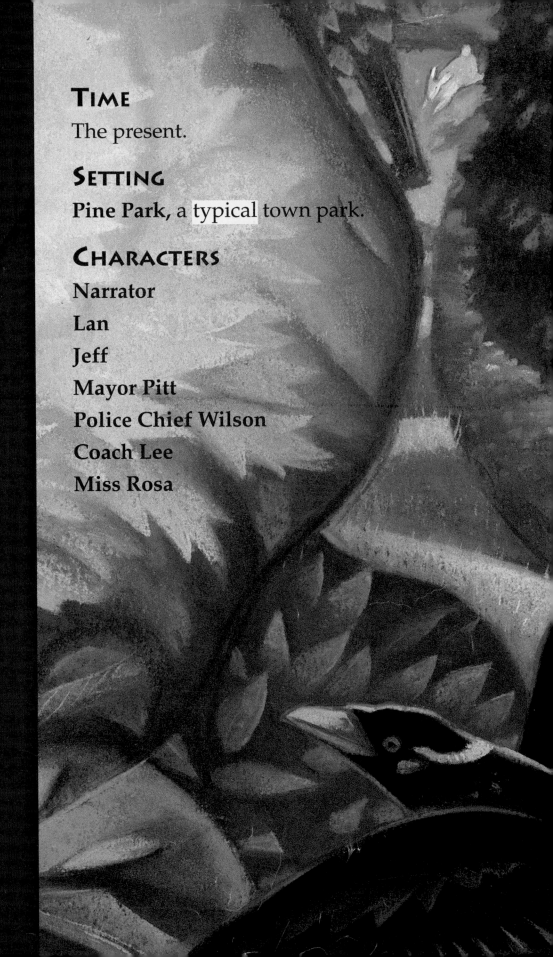

TIME

The present.

SETTING

Pine Park, a typical town park.

CHARACTERS

Narrator

Lan

Jeff

Mayor Pitt

Police Chief Wilson

Coach Lee

Miss Rosa

Genre

Play

A play is a story that can be acted out.

Look for

- **words that tell the characters' actions and feelings.**
- **a plot divided into scenes.**

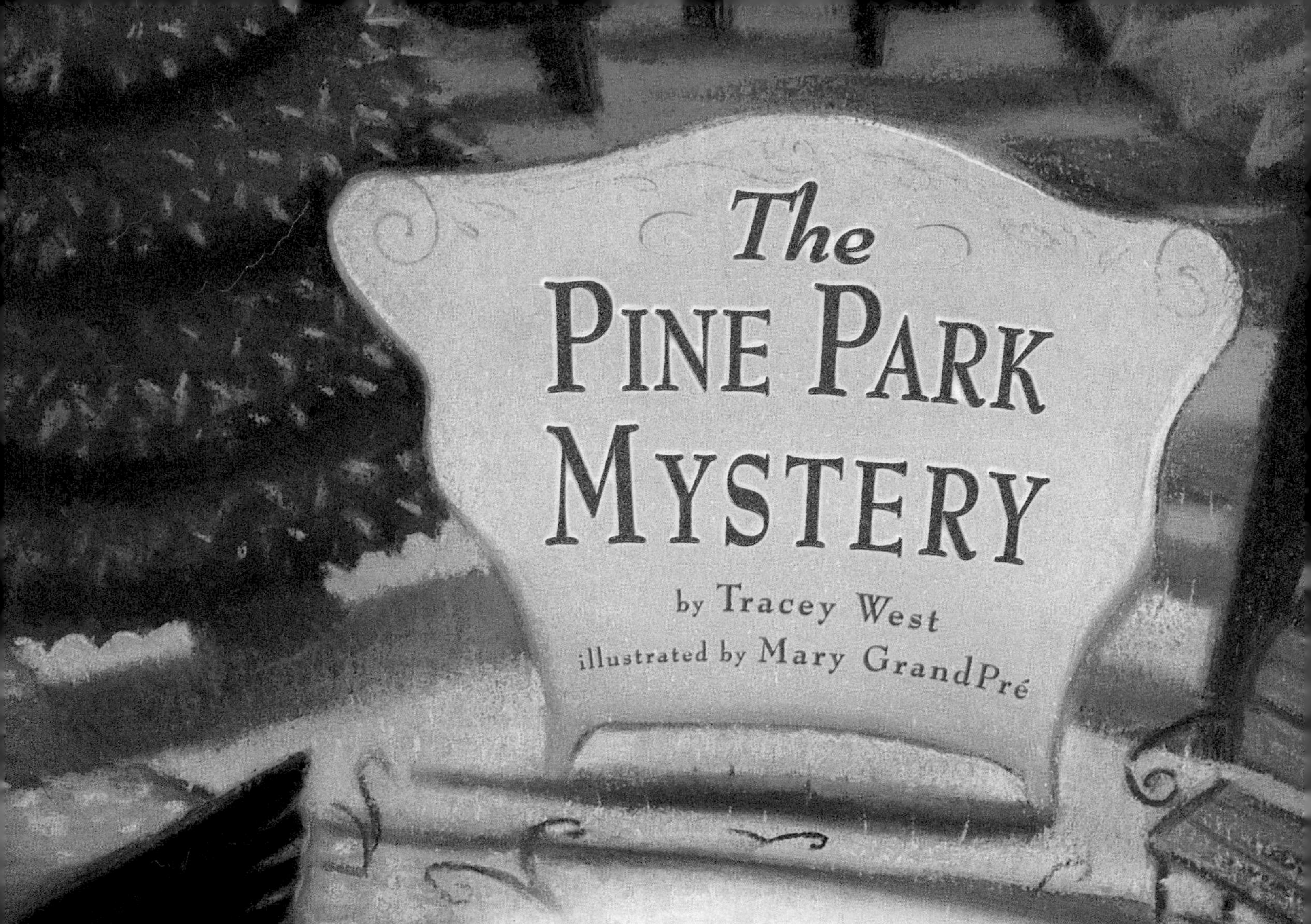

The PINE PARK MYSTERY

by Tracey West

illustrated by Mary GrandPré

SCENE ONE

Narrator: It is a beautiful afternoon in Pine Park. The sun is shining, and the birds are singing. It's just another ordinary day... or is it?

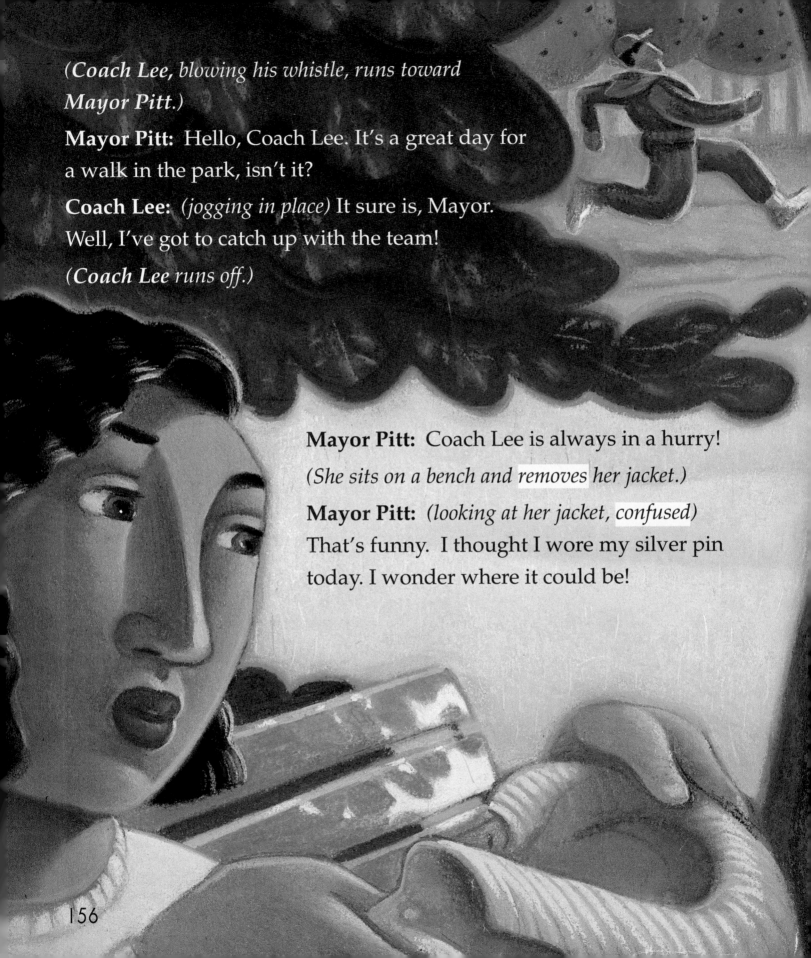

(*Coach Lee, blowing his whistle, runs toward Mayor Pitt.*)

Mayor Pitt: Hello, Coach Lee. It's a great day for a walk in the park, isn't it?

Coach Lee: (*jogging in place*) It sure is, Mayor. Well, I've got to catch up with the team!

(*Coach Lee runs off.*)

Mayor Pitt: Coach Lee is always in a hurry!

(*She sits on a bench and removes her jacket.*)

Mayor Pitt: (*looking at her jacket, confused*) That's funny. I thought I wore my silver pin today. I wonder where it could be!

Narrator: In another part of the park, Lan and Jeff are playing catch.

Lan: I'm bored. Nothing exciting ever seems to happen around here.

(*Jeff* tosses the ball to *Lan*.)

Jeff: You're always bored. Isn't playing catch in the park enough fun for you?

(*Lan* catches the ball and then drops it suddenly, looking confused. She looks closely at her wrist.)

Lan: That's funny. My charm bracelet is missing. The clasp was loose. . . .

Jeff: Maybe it fell off near here. Let's look.

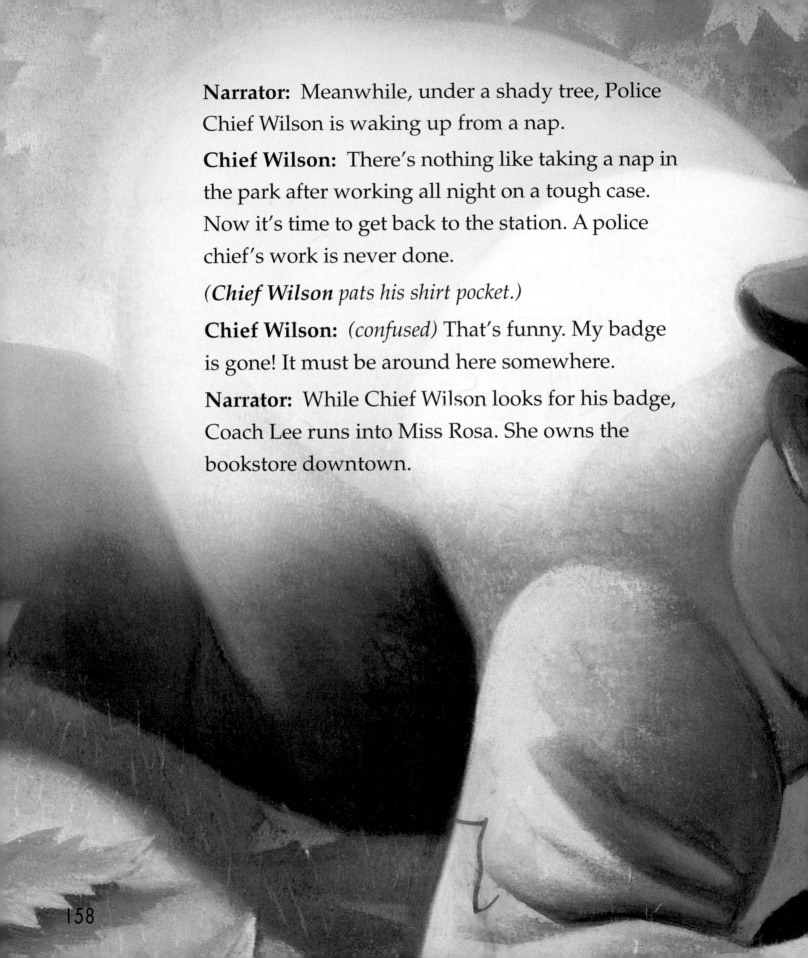

Narrator: Meanwhile, under a shady tree, Police Chief Wilson is waking up from a nap.

Chief Wilson: There's nothing like taking a nap in the park after working all night on a tough case. Now it's time to get back to the station. A police chief's work is never done.

(**Chief Wilson** *pats his shirt pocket.*)

Chief Wilson: *(confused)* That's funny. My badge is gone! It must be around here somewhere.

Narrator: While Chief Wilson looks for his badge, Coach Lee runs into Miss Rosa. She owns the bookstore downtown.

Miss Rosa: Hi, Coach. Where are you running to?

Coach Lee: I'm trying to find my whistle. I had it a few minutes ago, but now I can't find it anywhere.

Miss Rosa: That's funny—I'm looking for something, too.

Narrator: Is something mysterious happening in Pine Park? Lan and Jeff are about to find out.

SCENE TWO

Narrator: Lan and Jeff see Chief Wilson posting a sign on a tree.

Jeff: *(reading)* Missing: One police badge, one silver pin, and one whistle.

Lan: You can add one charm bracelet to that list, Chief.

Chief Wilson: *(scratching his head)* It's the strangest thing. I can't figure out why all these objects are missing. It's a real mystery.

Lan: A mystery! Now *that* sounds exciting.

SCENE THREE

Narrator: Lan and Jeff are about to try to solve the case of the missing objects.

Lan: We have to think like real detectives, Jeff. Let's start by listing what we know about this case.

Jeff: Well, everyone noticed the objects were missing while he or she was in the park.

Lan: That's right. What else do we know?

Jeff: All of the objects were pretty small . . . they were all shiny, too.

Lan: I have an idea! Let's put another small, shiny object in the park. Then we can hide and see what happens to it.

Jeff: How about the key to my bicycle lock?

(*Jeff takes the key from his pocket and puts it on a nearby rock. Jeff and Lan hide behind a tree. A group of kids runs across the stage, blocking the audience's view of the key on the rock.*)

Narrator: There goes Coach Lee's team. But look! The key is gone!

163

SCENE FOUR

(*Lan* leads *Chief Wilson*, *Mayor Pitt*, *Coach Lee*, and *Miss Rosa* to a tree in the park, where *Jeff* is waiting for them.)

Lan: *(to Jeff)* Do you have the thief cornered?

Jeff: *(smiling)* She's up in that tree.

Coach Lee: *(jogging in place)* Thief? I don't see anybody in that tree.

Chief Wilson: *(peers into the tree and smiles)* The thief isn't any*body*, Coach. It's a bird!

Miss Rosa: *(gasps)* That's Dynah! She's my new pet mynah bird. She escaped from the bookstore this morning. I've been looking for her all day! *(looks at **Lan** and **Jeff**)* How did you two know Dynah was the thief?

165

Lan: Jeff figured out that all the missing objects were small and shiny, so we decided to set a trap. We put Jeff's bicycle key on a rock. Dynah flew by and picked it up.

Jeff: Then she flew into this tree.

Miss Rosa: Mynah birds do like to collect shiny objects. I'll bet you'll find all the missing things somewhere in the tree.

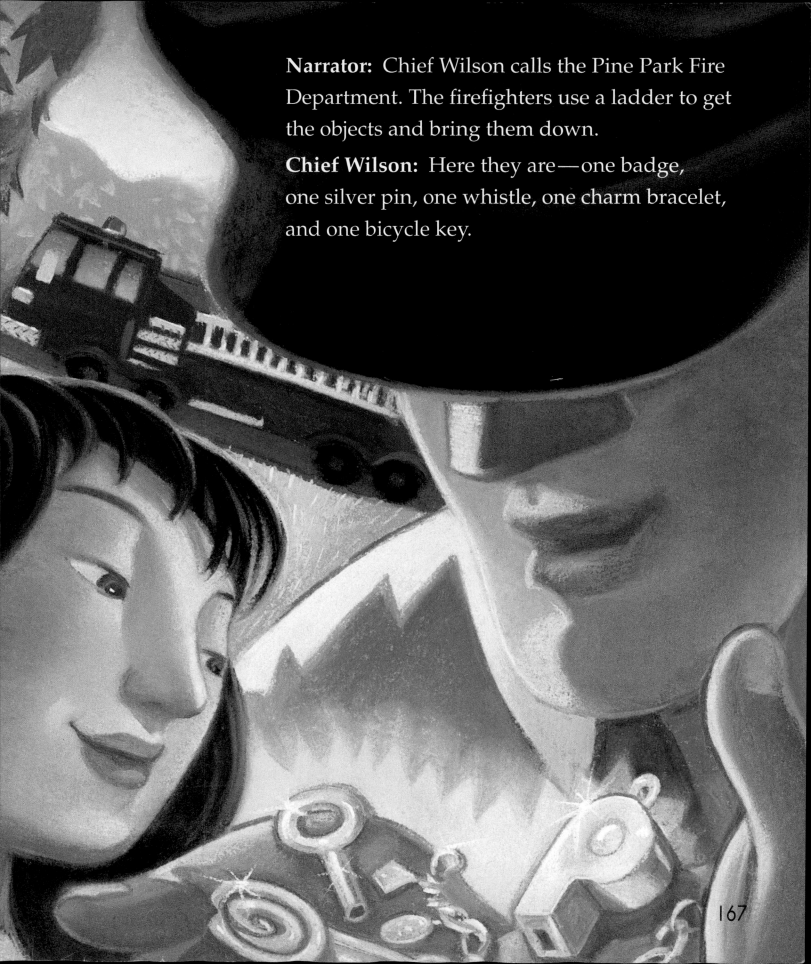

Narrator: Chief Wilson calls the Pine Park Fire Department. The firefighters use a ladder to get the objects and bring them down.

Chief Wilson: Here they are—one badge, one silver pin, one whistle, one charm bracelet, and one bicycle key.

167

Miss Rosa: *(holding a bird cage with Dynah in it)* I'm sorry Dynah caused so much trouble, Mayor Pitt. I'll try to keep a close eye on her from now on.

Mayor Pitt: *(laughing)* She certainly caused quite a stir! A day in Pine Park was never so exciting.

Lan: I can't wait to come back to the park tomorrow!

Jeff: To play catch?

Lan: No, I want to see if there's another mystery we can solve!

THINK AND RESPOND

1. What is the mystery in Pine Park?

2. Where in the play did you find out what **caused** this mystery? Why?

3. What clues helped you solve the mystery?

4. What part of the play did you like best?

5. What strategies helped you read this play?

Visit *The Learning Site!*
www.harcourtschool.com

Tracey West   *Mary GrandPré*

MEET THE AUTHOR

Tracey West loved reading so much as a child that she decided she wanted to be an author. She writes at her home near New York City, where she lives with her husband, her dog, Tisha, and her cat, Elvira.

MEET THE ILLUSTRATOR

Mary GrandPré has illustrated many children's books and made artwork for an animated film. She lives in St. Paul, Minnesota.

Birds D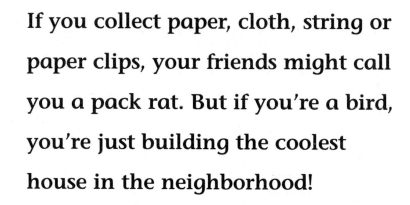o It! Recycle!

If you collect paper, cloth, string or paper clips, your friends might call you a pack rat. But if you're a bird, you're just building the coolest house in the neighborhood!

You can make a collection box of stuff to leave for birds so they can help themselves. Hang a small plastic box with holes (like the ones berries come in) on a tree branch. Stuff the box loosely with nest-building goodies. Hang the box on a tree and watch birds climb on board to pick through the junk to find their treasures.

Look and see how your old junk can help decorate and warm a bird's new home.

Worn-out shoelaces work well to keep a nest snug and warm.

Bits of cotton help keep a nest warm and cozy.

Birds like yarn. Make sure the strings are no longer than six inches. Otherwise, birds may get tangled up in them and get hurt.

Rags are great. Try to give birds strips of cloth made of natural fibers.

Think and Respond

What things can you do in your community to help nature?

Making Connections

Compare Texts

1 Why do you think "The Pine Park Mystery" is in a theme called Neighborhood News?

2 Think about two characters in "The Pine Park Mystery" who have community jobs. Tell how their jobs are alike and different.

3 In "Birds Do It! Recycle!" you read about things that birds collect for building their nests. How are the objects that Dynah picks up different?

Write a Scene

Jimmy: Hi, Dave. Do you want to go to the park?

Dave: Sure! What should I bring?

Jimmy: Bring a baseball and your glove.

Dave: Okay! Let's meet on the corner right away.

Think of a time you talked with a friend. Write what each of you said, as a scene in a play. With a classmate, read your scene with feeling.

Writing CONNECTION

Bird-Watching

To find out about birds in your community, make a bird feeder to hang near your house or classroom. Draw and write about the kinds of birds that come to eat from your feeder.

Science CONNECTION

Meet the Mayor

You have a mayor in your city or town. Find out your mayor's name and write it. Then list the jobs you know about that your mayor does to help your community.

Social Studies CONNECTION

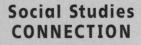

Narrative Elements

Every story has a setting, characters, and a plot. The **plot** is what happens during the beginning, middle, and end of a story. The beginning tells about a problem. The middle tells how the characters deal with it. The end tells how they solve it.

A story map shows the plot of a story. Look at this story map for "The Pine Park Mystery." What would you write in the last box?

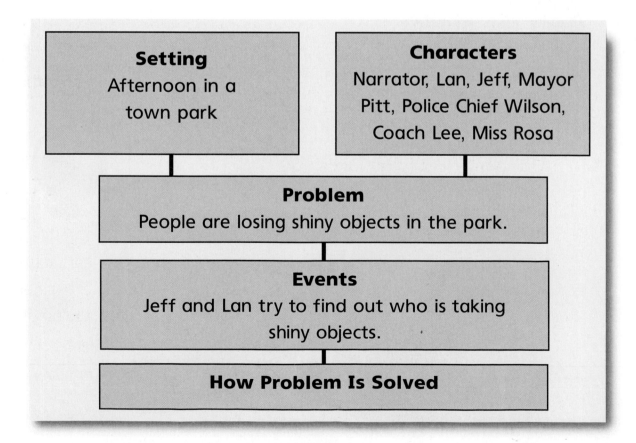

Setting
Afternoon in a
town park

Characters
Narrator, Lan, Jeff, Mayor
Pitt, Police Chief Wilson,
Coach Lee, Miss Rosa

Problem
People are losing shiny objects in the park.

Events
Jeff and Lan try to find out who is taking
shiny objects.

How Problem Is Solved

Focus Skill

Read the story. Then answer the questions.

A Day at the Park

The town park was a mess. Jason wanted to clean it up, but he could not do it alone. He asked his friends and neighbors to meet at the park on Saturday. They all worked together to pick up trash, paint the benches, and trim the bushes. Now everyone can enjoy the park.

1. **In this story's plot, what is the problem?**
   - ○ The park is closed.
   - ○ The park is a mess.
   - ○ People clean the park.
   - ○ Jason needs a friend.

Tip
Reread the beginning of the story to help you find the answer.

2. **How is the problem solved?**
   - ○ Jason finds people to help clean the park.
   - ○ People stop using the park on Saturdays.
   - ○ The mayor cleans the park.
   - ○ Jason cleans the park alone on Sunday.

Tip
Carefully read each answer choice before you choose the correct answer.

▲ Good-bye, Curtis

addresses

clerk

grown

honor

pour

route

Vocabulary Power

Hundreds of letters **pour** into your post office each day.

The **clerk** who works at the post office sorts the letters by their street **addresses**.

Each letter has a stamp. Some stamps **honor** famous people by showing their faces.

Letter carriers deliver the letters to homes and businesses every day. The path they follow is called a mail **route**.

The United States Postal Service has **grown** very large. Now it is one of the biggest and best postal systems in the world.

Good-bye,
Curtis

KEVIN HENKES
ARISABINA RUSSO

Award-Winning
Author

Genre

Realistic Fiction

Realistic fiction is a story that can happen in the real world.

Look for

- story events that can happen in real life.

- characters that act in ways they might act in the real world.

FIRST CLASS

PARIS BX ARTS
18 H
93
1995
R DES ST PERES

Good-

by Kevin Henkes

bye, Curtis

pictures by Marisabina Russo

Curtis has been a letter carrier

for forty-two years.

Today is his last day.

Everyone loves Curtis —

the old woman on the hill,

the baby in 4-C,

the clerk at the butcher shop,

and the crossing guard

at the corner of First and Park.

All of the mailboxes all over his route are filled

with all kinds of surprises. There is a chocolate

cupcake with sprinkles from Mrs. Martin.

There is a drawing from Debbie,

Dennis, and Donny.

There is a bottle of aftershave from

the Johnsons, and a box of nuts

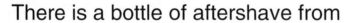

from their dog.

There are cards

and candy and cookies.

There are hugs and

handshakes and kisses.

There is a small, fat book from

Mr. Porter, and a pencil sharpener

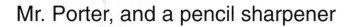

in the shape of a mailbox from Max.

"We'll miss you, Curtis,"

say the old woman on the hill

and the baby in 4-C

and the clerk at the butcher shop

and the crossing guard

at the corner of First and Park.

The children Curtis met when

he first began his route have

grown up.

Some of them have children of their own.

Some of them have grandchildren.

Some of the children have had

dogs. Some of the dogs have had puppies.

Cats have had kittens, too.

Trees have grown from little to big.

Houses have been torn down. And houses have

gone up. People have moved out.

And people have moved in.

But everyone loves Curtis.
"We'll miss you," they all say.
The dogs and cats say so, too.

When Curtis gets to the last mailbox
at the last house on the last street . . .

Surprise! Surprise! Surprise!

Curtis's own family is waiting there.
Friends pour out the door and down the steps.
People from all over his route run out from
the backyard.

They have a party in Curtis's honor.
"We love you, Curtis," they all say.
"We'll miss you."

There is dancing and eating and
remembering. There are balloons and
streamers and tiny tin horns.

That night Curtis dreams of his party.
When he wakes up the next morning,
he begins writing thank-you notes to everyone.

And he knows all the addresses by heart.

Think and Respond

1 What changes has Curtis seen during his forty-two years as a letter carrier?

2 How is the setting important in this story?

3 How do the author and illustrator show that the people on Curtis's **route** care about him?

4 Would you like to live along Curtis's route? Why or why not?

5 What strategies did you use to read this story?

Meet the Author
Kevin Henkes

Dear Readers,

When I was your age, I loved to go to the library. I carried all my books home by myself, no matter how many I had. I think my visits to the library helped me decide to become an author.

I like to end my stories in a hopeful way. Reading a story with a hopeful ending is like coming home from school and putting on play clothes. It feels good!

Kevin Henkes

Meet the Illustrator
Marisabina Russo

Dear Readers,

When I was a child, I drew pictures all the time. I especially liked to draw pictures of children and dogs. Once I got into trouble for drawing on the bottom of a table. After that my mother gave me a new pad of paper every week.

Marisab Russo

Visit *The Learning Site!*
www.harcourtschool.com

195

Making Connections

Compare Texts

1 How is Curtis a special part of his neighborhood?

2 What is the setting of this story? Compare it to the setting of "The Pine Park Mystery."

3 Tell about some of the characters in this story besides Curtis. How do you think they feel about Curtis? How do you know?

Letter of Introduction

Imagine that you have just found a pen pal—a new friend to write to in a faraway place. Write a letter about yourself that Curtis could deliver with other mail. In your letter, give your name and tell what you like to do.

Writing
CONNECTION

Personal Time Line

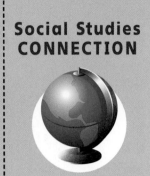

Curtis has had a long and busy life. Make a time line of your own life. List important things that have happened in your life and the years when they happened. Show them in the right order.

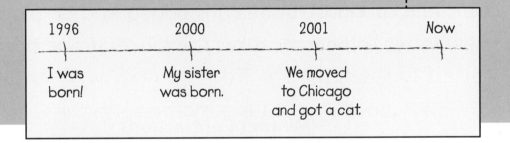

1996	2000	2001	Now
I was born!	My sister was born.	We moved to Chicago and got a cat.	

Stamp Sense

Find out how much it costs to buy one stamp for a letter. How much does it cost to buy two stamps? Three stamps? Share your information with the class. Explain how you found your answers.

▲ Good-bye, Curtis

Contractions:
'll, n't, 's

Sometimes, when you use two words together, you can make them into one word. These new words are called **contractions**. One or more letters are taken out, and an **apostrophe (')** is added in their place. A new letter sometimes takes the place of one or more letters.

Writing Contractions	
Contractions with 'll	**Contractions with n't**
we will ⟶ we'll they will ⟶ they'll	do not ⟶ don't can not ⟶ can't
Contractions with 's	**Contractions That Change Spelling**
let us ⟶ let's he is ⟶ he's	will not ⟶ won't

Make the contractions in each of these sentences.

I am going to the party.

They will not come with me.

She is going to the post office.

198

Test Prep

Contractions: 'll, n't, 's

Choose the word that is the correct contraction for the underlined words.

Example: <u>did not</u>

- ○ did'nt
- ○ didnt
- ● didn't
- ○ dident

Tip

Skip over any choice that does not have an apostrophe.

1. <u>they will</u>

- ○ they'ill
- ○ they"ll
- ○ thell
- ○ they'll

2. <u>she is</u>

- ○ she'is
- ○ she's
- ○ she"is
- ○ shee's

3. <u>will not</u>

- ○ willn't
- ○ will'nt
- ○ wo'nt
- ○ won't

Tip

Remember that the apostrophe comes between the *n* and the *t*.

▲ Max Found
Two Sticks

appeared

conductor

created

imitated

rhythm

startled

Vocabulary Power

Alex waited with his father at the train station. He **created** a drum set from boxes to pass the time.

Alex could see the train coming. He listened to the **rhythm** in the sound of the wheels against the tracks. He **imitated** it on his boxes. *Rat-tat, rat-tat.*

Suddenly a loud whistle **startled** Alex. He jumped up in surprise.

Tickets, please!

The train **conductor** soon **appeared** at an open door. Alex and his dad gave him their tickets and climbed aboard.

Vocabulary-Writing CONNECTION

Write about a time that you **imitated** someone or something. Tell how you did it.

Genre

Realistic Fiction

Realistic fiction tells about events that could happen in real life.

Look for

- **characters that do things real people do.**

- **a setting that could be a real place.**

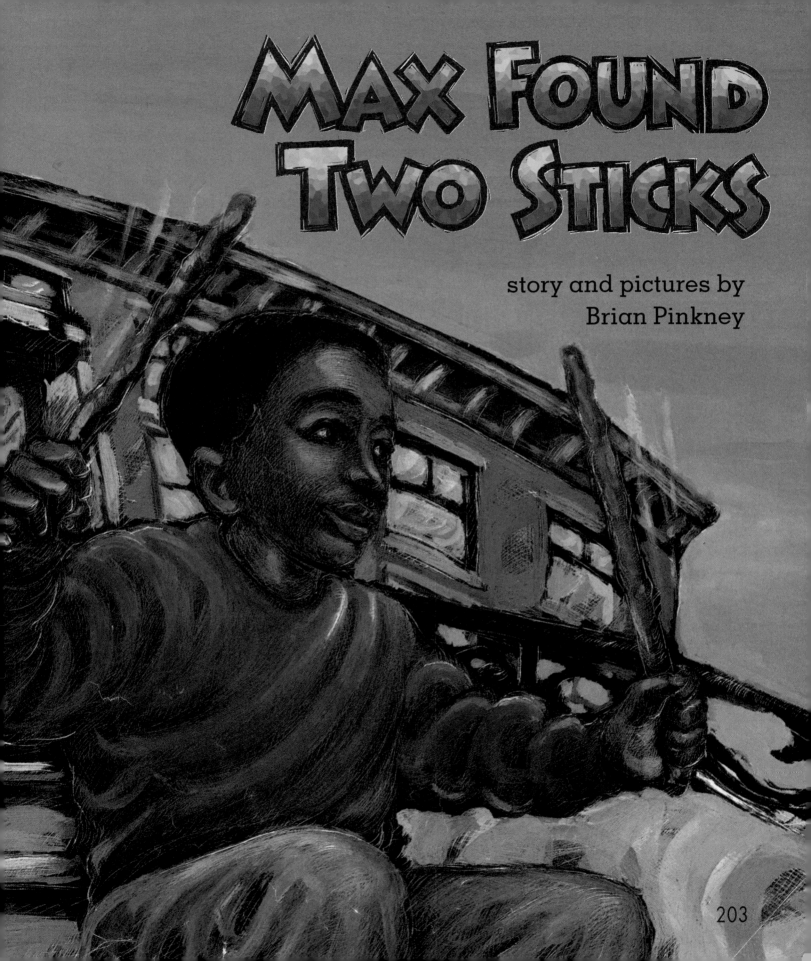

Max Found Two Sticks

story and pictures by
Brian Pinkney

It was a day when Max didn't feel like talking to anyone. He just sat on his front steps and watched the clouds gather in the sky.

A strong breeze shook the tree in front of his house, and Max saw two heavy twigs fall to the ground.

"What are you gonna do with those sticks?" Max's grandpa asked as he washed the front windows.

Not saying a word, Max tapped on his thighs, *Pat . . . pat-tat. Putter-putter . . . pat-tat.* His rhythm imitated the sound of the pigeons, startled into flight.

When Max's mother came home carrying new hats for his twin sisters, she asked, "What are you doing with Grandpa's cleaning bucket, Son?"

Max responded by patting the bucket, *Tap-tap-tap.*

207

Tippy-tip . . . *tat-tat*. He **created** the rhythm of the light rain falling against the front windows.

After a while the clouds moved on and the sun appeared. Cindy, Shaun and Jamal showed up drinking sodas. "Hey, Max! Whatcha doin' with those hatboxes?"

Again Max didn't answer. He just played on the boxes, *Dum . . . dum-de-dum.*

Di-di-di-di. Dum-dum. Max drummed the beat of the tom-toms in a marching band.

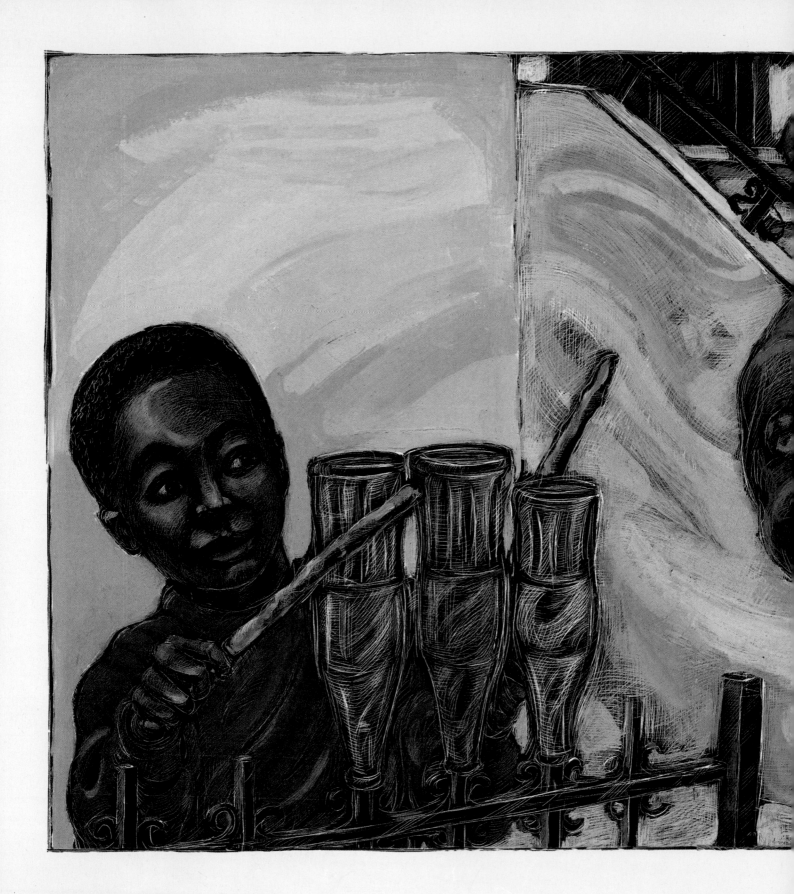

"What are you up to with those soda bottles?" his dad asked as he brought out the garbage cans on his way to work.

Max answered on the bottles, *Dong . . . dang . . . dung.*

Ding . . . dong . . . ding! His music joined the chiming of the bells in the church around the corner.

Soon the twins came out to show off their new hats. "Hey, Max," they asked, "what are you doin' with those garbage cans?"

Max hammered out a reply on the cans, *Cling . . . clang . . . da-BANG!*

A-cling-clang . . . DA-BANGGGG! Max pounded out the sound of the wheels thundering down the tracks under the train on which his father worked as a conductor.

Suddenly Max heard *Thump-di-di-thump . . . THUMP-DI-DI-THUMP!* as a marching band rounded the corner.

Max watched the drummers with amazement as they passed, copying their rhythms. The last drummer saw Max. Then with a nod and a wink, he tossed Max his spare set of sticks.

"Thanks," called Max—and he didn't miss a beat.

Think and Respond

1 What things does Max tap on to create **rhythm**?

2 How might the story be different if Max lived in the country instead of in the city?

3 How does Max feel at the beginning of the story? How does he feel at the end?

4 What is your favorite part of the story? Why?

5 What strategies helped you read this story?

BRIAN PINKNEY

What made you decide to write this book?

I wanted to write a book about drumming because I've played the drums most of my life. I almost made music my career. I had ideas about a book, but I didn't really have a story. I would jot down notes about a boy and how he liked to drum. It took me about four years to finish the book. I decided to start with the pictures. I would draw a little and then write a little. Most of the words came to me when I was just waking up in the morning or when I was away from my studio.

Visit *The Learning Site!*
www.harcourtschool.com

221

Snap your fingers.
Tap your feet.
Step out a rhythm
down the street.

Rap on a litter bin.
Stamp on the ground.
City music
is all around.

Beep says motor-car.
Ding says bike.
City music
is what we like.

by Tony Mitton

Making Connections

Compare Texts

1 Think about the settings in "Max Found Two Sticks," "Good-bye, Curtis," and "The Pine Park Mystery." How do these settings fit into this theme?

2 Why might Brian Pinkney have written "Max Found Two Sticks" as a story rather than as a play?

3 How is the poem "City Music" like "Max Found Two Sticks"?

What Happens Next?

What do you think Max will do with his new drumsticks? Use a web to list your ideas. Then write a story to tell what Max does next.

Writing
CONNECTION

Max has new drumsticks.

Sounds All Around

Max made music with objects he found. You can, too. Find things you can use to make interesting sounds. You might use sticks with boxes, cans, and other things. As you make different sounds, compare their loudness, or *volume*.

Science CONNECTION

All Aboard!

Imagine that you are a train conductor. Look at a map to find a place to travel to in your train. Will you travel to a city or the countryside? Brainstorm a list of the sights and sounds you might expect when you arrive.

Social Studies CONNECTION

Multiple-Meaning Words

Words that are spelled the same but have different meanings are called **multiple-meaning words.** Below is a multiple-meaning word from "Max Found Two Sticks." You can figure out its meanings from the ways it is used in the following sentences.

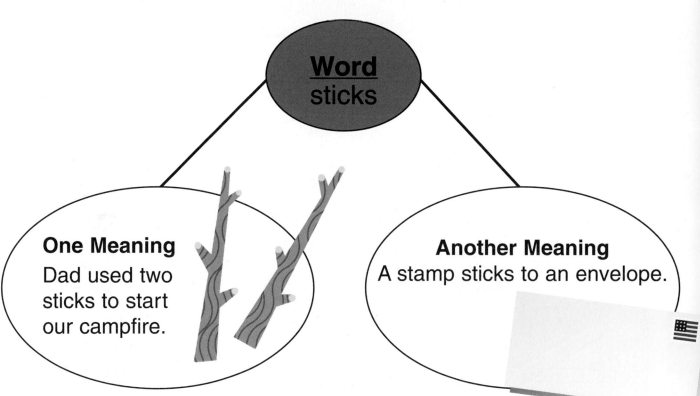

Word
sticks

One Meaning
Dad used two sticks to start our campfire.

Another Meaning
A stamp sticks to an envelope.

Visit *The Learning Site!*
www.harcourtschool.com

See *Skills* and *Activities*

The word *saw* is another multiple-meaning word from the story. What are its two meanings?

226

Test Prep

Multiple-Meaning Words

GEORGIA CRCT Tested Skill

Read the paragraph. Then complete the sentences.

Last Weekend

We went to the fair last weekend. We went on rides, played games, and stood in lines with lots of people. What I liked best was the band. It played jazz music all day long.

---

1. **In the paragraph above, the word** *fair* **means—**
   - ○ nice, warm weather
   - ○ honest and even
   - ○ an event with rides and games
   - ○ not too bad

   Tip Choose the answer that goes with the meaning in the paragraph.

2. **In this story, the word** *band* **is —**
   - ○ a piece of rubber used to hold things together
   - ○ a group of people who play music together
   - ○ a stripe of bright color
   - ○ a group of people who live together

   Tip Think about the meaning in the paragraph before you choose an answer.

Vocabulary Power

▲ Anthony Reynoso:
Born to Rope

dappled

exhibition

landscape
business

ranch

thousands

Each year, my family goes to the county fair. It is crowded with **thousands** of people. They come to look at animals, see arts and crafts, and eat delicious food.

My dad takes a day off to take us to the fair. He works for a **landscape business**. His job is to care for people's lawns and keep them looking good!

228

When we go to the fair, the first thing we do is look at the horses. They come from a nearby **ranch** that raises horses and cattle.

This is my favorite horse, Daisy. She has a beautiful **dappled** coat with brown spots on white. I come to see her every year.

A great part of the day is the talent **exhibition**. We watch people show off their special skills.

Vocabulary-Writing CONNECTION

Have you ever been to a place where there were **thousands** of people? Tell about the place and why so many people were there.

Genre

Nonfiction: Personal Narrative

A personal narrative is a true story about something important to the narrator.

Look for

- information about the narrator's life.

- first-person words such as *I*, *me*, and *my*.

Anthony Reynoso:

BORN TO ROPE

by Martha Cooper & Ginger Gordon

My name is Anthony Reynoso. I'm named after
my father, who is holding the white horse, and my
grandfather, who is holding the dappled horse.
We all rope and ride Mexican Rodeo style on my
grandfather's ranch outside of Phoenix, Arizona.

As soon as I could stand, my dad gave me a rope. I had my own little hat and everything else I needed to dress as a *charro*. That's what a Mexican cowboy is called. It's a good thing I started when I was little, because it takes years to learn to rope.

I live with my mom and dad in the little
Mexican-American and Yaqui Indian town of
Guadalupe. All my grandparents live close by.
This will help a lot when the new baby comes.
My mom is pregnant.

I've got a secret about Guadalupe. I know where there are petroglyphs in the rocks right near my house. My favorite looks like a man with a shield. People carved these petroglyphs hundreds of years ago. Why did they do it? I wonder what the carvings mean.

Every Sunday morning the old Mexican Mission church is packed. At Easter, lots of people come to watch the Yaqui Indian ceremonies in the center of town.

Some Sundays, we go to Casa Reynoso, my grandparents' restaurant. If it's very busy, my cousins and I pitch in. When there's time, my grandmother lets me help in the kitchen. Casa Reynoso has the best Mexican food in town.

On holidays, we go to my grandfather's ranch. Once a year, we all get dressed up for a family photo.

I've got lots of cousins. Whenever there's a birthday we have a piñata. We smash it with a stick until all the candy falls out. Then we scramble to grab as much as we can hold.

Best of all, at the ranch we get to practice roping on horseback. My dad's always trying something new . . . and so am I!

In Mexico, the Rodeo is the national sport. The most famous charros there are like sports stars here.

On weekdays, Dad runs his landscape business,
Mom works in a public school, and I go to school.
I wait for the bus with other kids at the corner
of my block.

I always come to school with
my homework done. When I'm
in class, I forget about roping
and riding. I don't think anyone
in school knows about it except
my best friends.

It's different when I get home. I practice hard with Dad. He's a good teacher and shows me everything his father taught him. We spend a lot of time practicing for shows at schools, malls, and rodeos. We are experts at passing the rope. Our next big exhibition is in Sedona, about two hours away by car.

After rope practice we shoot a few baskets. Dad's pretty good at that too!

On Friday after school, Dad and I prepare our ropes for the show in Sedona. They've got to be just right.

Everything's ready for tomorrow, so I can take a break and go through my basketball cards. I decide which ones I want to buy, sell, and trade. Collecting basketball cards is one of my favorite hobbies.

It's Saturday! Time for the show in Sedona. I get a little nervous watching the other performers. I sure wouldn't want to get messed up in my own rope in front of all these people! After the Mexican hat dance, we're next!

My dad goes first . . . and then it's my turn. While the mariachis play, I do my stuff. Even Dad can't spin the rope from his teeth like this!

Then Dad and I rope together, just like we practiced. It's hard to do with our wide charro hats on. When my dad passes the rope to me and I spin it well, he says he has passed the Mexican Rodeo tradition on to me. Now it's up to me to keep it going.

Mom is our best fan. She always comes with us. It makes me feel good to know she's out there watching.

Sometimes tourists want us to pose for pictures with them. It makes me feel like a celebrity.

After the show, boy, are we hungry! We pack up and eat a quick lunch. Then we go to a special place called Slide Rock. Slide Rock is a natural water slide where kids have played for hundreds, maybe even thousands, of years. It's cold today! I'd rather come back in the summer when it's hot. But Dad pulls me in anyway. Brrr!

Time to go home. Next time we come to Sedona, the baby will be with us. I wonder if it will be a boy or a girl. It's hard to wait! I'm going to love being a big brother. Pretty soon the baby will be wearing my old boots and learning how to rope from me.

THINK AND RESPOND

❶ What does Anthony tell you about his life in a Mexican-American family?

❷ Why do you think the authors wrote about Anthony Reynoso?

❸ Why do Anthony and his father rope and ride Mexican Rodeo style?

❹ What skill would you like to learn? What kind of **exhibition** might you give to show off your skill?

❺ What strategies helped you read this selection?

MEET THE AUTHORS

Ginger Gordon is a first-grade teacher and a writer. She has written another book with Martha Cooper called *My Two Worlds.* That book is about an eight-year-old girl who lives in both New York City and the Dominican Republic. Ginger Gordon likes to show what life is like for children in different cultures.

Martha Cooper is a photographer. She likes to show how people from many different backgrounds live together in neighborhoods. Her photographs can be found in magazines, books, calendars, and museum shows. Martha Cooper lives in New York City.

**Visit *The Learning Site!*
www.harcourtschool.com**

Making Connections

Compare Texts

1   Why do you think "Anthony Reynoso: Born to Rope" is part of the Neighborhood News theme?

2   Who is speaking in this selection? How does this way of telling a story differ from "Max Found Two Sticks"?

3   How is the main character in this story like the main character in "Max Found Two Sticks"?

In the Family

Write a paragraph to tell what things Anthony's parents do to help him be a good roper. Make a list of examples from the story to help you plan your paragraph.

Writing
CONNECTION

Local Weather

The weather in your area can be very different from the weather in another place. Use a newspaper to keep track of the temperature in a city that is far away for two weeks. Use a thermometer to record your local temperature. Compare the temperatures by using a chart like this one.

Temperature			
Place	May 18	May 23	May 28
Phoenix	70°	80°	88°
My Home	65°	70°	75°

Map Search

Use a map of North America to find Arizona, Anthony's home. Then find Mexico, the place where Anthony's family came from. Find the names of the states closest to Arizona. Then share your information with the class.

▲ **Anthony Reynoso: Born to Rope**

Words with *gh* and *ph*

Phonics Skill

Read these sentences about Anthony Reynoso.

Anthony gets dressed up for a <u>photo</u>.
He <u>laughs</u> when his dad pulls him into the water.

Say the underlined words, *photo* and *laughs*. Listen for the "f" sound in each word. In these words, the letters **gh** or **ph** stand for the "f" sound.

Look at the next two words. What do you notice about *graph* and *cough* that could help you read the words?

graph   cough

Here are some longer words. Use what you know about **gh** and **ph** to sound them out. What do all these words have in common?

toughen	**coughing**	**graphed**
alphabet	**photographer**	**laughing**

Use these tips to read a longer word.
• Look for word parts you know.
• Break the word into parts.
• Say each part. Then blend the parts and say the word.

Test Prep

Words with *gh* and *ph*

GEORGIA
CRCT Tested Skill

Find the word that has the same sound as the underlined letters in the first word.

Example: <u>ph</u>oto

- ○ steep
- ○ post
- ● staff

Tip

Look at the underlined letters closely. Be sure you know the sound they make.

1. lau<u>gh</u>
   - ○ tricky
   - ○ alphabet
   - ○ grass

2. gra<u>ph</u>
   - ○ grin
   - ○ pass
   - ○ puffing

3. cou<u>gh</u>ing
   - ○ photograph
   - ○ creak
   - ○ gash

249

Vocabulary Power

▲ Chinatown

celebrations

develop

furious

graceful

grocery store

students

Baker Street Mall has many stores. Mom goes to Jack's Market. It is a **grocery store** that sells all kinds of food.

Grandpa and I watch the dance **students** practice. They are learning to be **graceful** as they move in beautiful ways. They practice to **develop** and build strong legs.

Dad is **furious** with himself. He is angry because he forgot to bring along the sweater he wanted to return.

My sister likes the party store. She looks at the things people use for birthdays and other **celebrations**.

Vocabulary-Writing CONNECTION

Write a short description of your favorite **celebration**. Tell when it is, what you do, and why you like it.

251

Genre

Realistic Fiction

Realistic fiction is a story with characters and events that are like people and events in real life.

Look for

- a setting that is a real place.
- story events that could really happen.

CHINATOWN

WRITTEN AND ILLUSTRATED BY

WILLIAM LOW

253

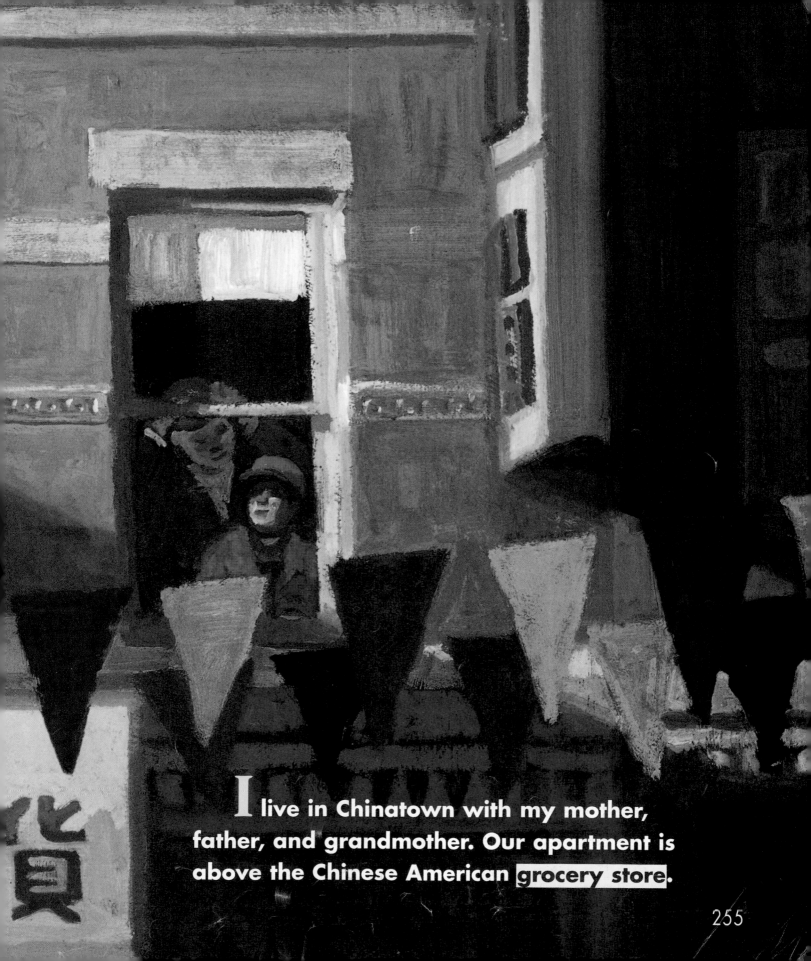

I live in Chinatown with my mother, father, and grandmother. Our apartment is above the Chinese American grocery store.

Every morning Grandma and I
go for a walk through Chinatown.
We hold hands before we cross
the street. "Watch out for cars,
Grandma," I tell her.

Most days the tai chi class has already begun by the time we get to the park. Students, young and old, move in the sunlight like graceful dancers.

We always stop and
say hello to Mr. Wong, the
street cobbler. If our shoes
need fixing, Mr. Wong can
do the job.

"Just like new, and at
a good price, too," says
Mr. Wong.

Chinatown really wakes up when the delivery trucks arrive. Men with handcarts move quickly over the sidewalks and into the stores.

Every day Grandma and I walk past the Dai-Dai Restaurant. Roasted chicken is my favorite, but Grandma likes duck best.

When it gets cold outside and
Grandma needs to make medicinal soup,
we visit the herbal shop. Inside it is dark
and smells musty. The owner, Mr. Chung,
is bagging dried roots and herbs.

"Winter is here," says Grandma. "We
must get our strength up."

Sometimes Grandma and I go for lunch at a seafood restaurant. I like to watch the fish swim in the tank. Grandma says, "You won't find fresher fish than those in Chinatown."

The kitchen in the restaurant is a noisy place. Hot oil sizzles, vegetables crackle, and woks clang and bang. The cooks shout to be heard.

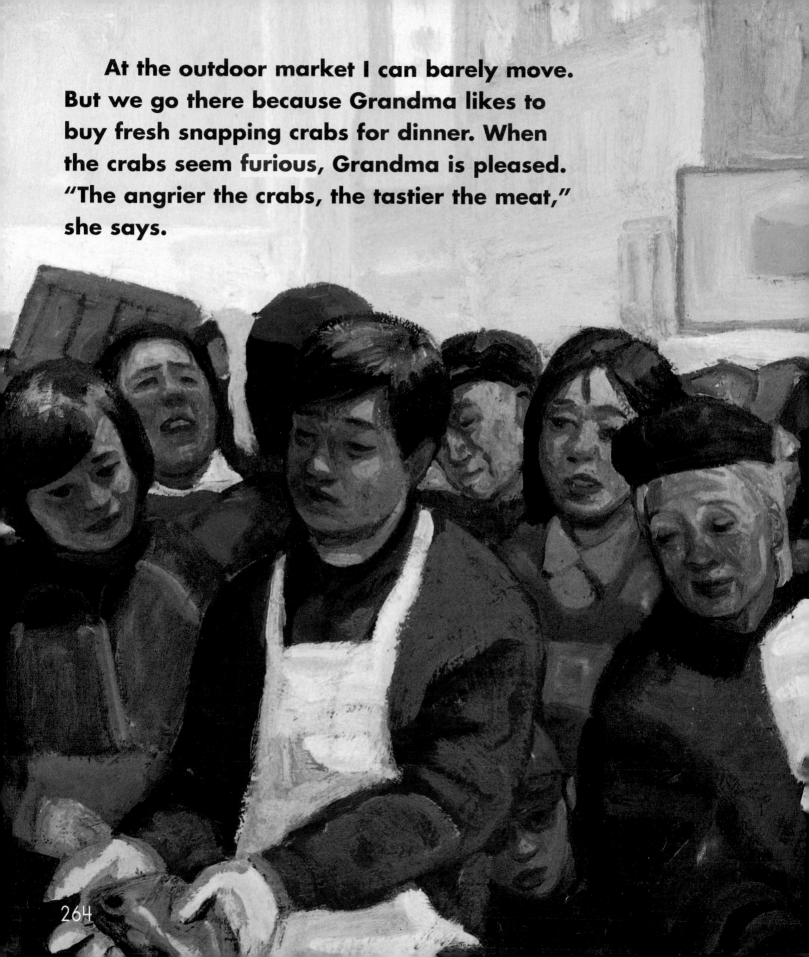

At the outdoor market I can barely move.
But we go there because Grandma likes to
buy fresh snapping crabs for dinner. When
the crabs seem furious, Grandma is pleased.
"The angrier the crabs, the tastier the meat,"
she says.

On Saturdays I take lessons at the kung fu school. Master Leung teaches us a new move each week. "To **develop** your body *and* your mind," says Master Leung, "you must practice every day."

My favorite holiday is Chinese New Year. During the **celebrations** the streets of Chinatown are always crowded. "Be sure to stay close by," Grandma says.

On New Year's Day the older kids from my kung fu school march to the beat of thumping drums. Grandma and I try to find a good place to watch, and I tell her that next year I'll be marching, too.

The New Year's Day parade winds noisily through the streets. "Look, Grandma!" I say. "Here comes the lion."

Firecrackers explode when the lion dance is over. I turn to Grandma, take her hand, and say, "Gung hay fat choy, Grandma."

She smiles at me. "And a happy new year to you, too."

Think and Respond

1. What do the boy and his grandmother see and do on their walk through Chinatown?

2. How does the author write about the setting?

3. How do you think the boy feels about Chinatown? Tell why you think as you do.

4. What **celebrations** do you enjoy most? Why?

5. What did you picture in your mind as you read this story?

MEET THE AUTHOR AND ILLUSTRATOR
WILLIAM LOW

William Low was born in New York City, but he never lived in Chinatown. He grew up in the Bronx and Queens, which are other parts of the city. When he was older, William Low climbed onto the roof of his parents' house and painted pictures of nearby buildings. Today, he teaches art at a school near Chinatown.

 Visit *The Learning Site!*
www.harcourtschool.com

Look What Came From
CHINA

by Miles Harvey

Children practicing kung fu

Sports and Exercise

Many of China's physical arts have made their way to the United States. One very famous Chinese sport is a special type of boxing known as *kung fu*. This sport is very difficult. To become good at it, you have to practice for many years.

Tai Chi

A popular kind of exercise in China is known as *tai chi*. It is very good for you. It is also very interesting to watch. People who do tai chi sometimes look as if they are dancing in slow motion.

For more than 2,000 years, people in China have been doing a sport called *acrobatics*. People who are acrobats perform amazing tricks. Some of them juggle things in the air. Others pile objects up very high and then balance themselves on top of these objects. No wonder people love to go see acrobats at the circus!

Chinese acrobats

273

Making Connections

Compare Texts

1 In this theme, which communities are most alike? Why?

2 How is the ending of "Chinatown" like the ending of "Max Found Two Sticks"?

3 Compare "Chinatown" to "Look What Came From China." Which selection gives more information about *kung fu* and *tai chi*?

Write About Your Neighborhood

The boy in "Chinatown" tells about the sights, sounds, and smells of his community. In your journal, write about the things you see, hear, and smell in your own neighborhood. Use describing words to add details.

Writing CONNECTION

> April 21, 2003
> Yesterday I went to the park with Grandpa. We saw Miss Perez playing with her dogs. The smallest dog jumped and barked.

Exercise Your Muscles

The boy in "Chinatown" says that people in the *tai chi* class move "like graceful dancers." Think about the steps to a dance or exercise that you like to do. Write notes. Then have a partner listen to your directions and follow them. Use words such as *up, down, around,* and *under*.

Getting What You Need

Think about the different kinds of stores where you live. Make a list of the ones your family needs. Then tell why each of these stores is important.

Details

Details are bits of information in a story or in other writing that tell more about something. Details help you picture what you read. They also make what you read more interesting.

Read the sentences below. How did the author use details to help you know more about each topic?

TOPIC	TOPIC **+** DETAILS
The kitchen in the restaurant is a noisy place.	The kitchen in the restaurant is a noisy place. Hot oil sizzles, vegetables crackle, and woks clang and bang. The cooks shout to be heard.
I live in Chinatown.	I live in Chinatown with my mother, father, and grandmother. Our apartment is above the Chinese American grocery store.

Chinatown

Read page 262 again. What details do you find?

Read the story. Then answer the questions.

Annie's New Hat

Annie bought a new hat. It was white with a yellow ribbon around it. On the ribbon were white daisies. The ribbon matched her new yellow dress perfectly.

1. **Annie's hat was—**
   ○ yellow
   ○ white
   ○ curly
   ○ old

Tip

As you read the story, note any details that are important.

2. **What kind of flowers were on Annie's hat?**
   ○ yellow daisies
   ○ white daisies
   ○ yellow tulips
   ○ white tulips

Tip

Reread the story to find the answer.

Travel TIME

CONTENTS

Vocabulary Power

flock

glide

harbor

soared

swooping

I live by a large harbor. A **harbor** is a place by the sea where boats can dock. It's also a great place to watch birds!

This morning I saw a **flock** of seagulls flying together. There must have been hundreds of them. They were **swooping** through the air, moving up and down and side to side.

I saw one seagull **glide** above the waves for a long time. The bird looked calm and peaceful as it flew.

Finally the bird **soared** up high and joined the others. I watched them fly away and wished that I could fly, too!

Vocabulary-Writing CONNECTION

Think about the way birds **glide** through the air. Write a short poem about how you think they feel.

281

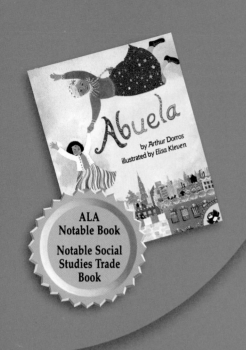

Genre

Fantasy

A fantasy is a story about events that can not happen in real life.

Look for

- characters who do things that real people can not do.

- a setting that may be different from the real world.

by Arthur Dorros

illustrated by Elisa Kleven

Abuela takes me on the bus. We go all around
the city.

Abuela is my grandma. She is my mother's mother.
Abuela means "grandma" in Spanish.
Abuela speaks mostly Spanish because that's what
people spoke where she grew up, before she came to
this country. Abuela and I are always going places.

Today we're going to the park.
"El parque es lindo," says Abuela.
I know what she means. I think the park is beautiful too.

"Tantos pájaros," Abuela says
as a flock of birds surrounds us.
So many birds. They're picking up the bread we brought.

What if they picked me up
and carried me
high above the park?
What if I could fly?
Abuela would wonder where I was.
Swooping like a bird, I'd call to her.

Then she'd see me flying.
Rosalba the bird.
"Rosalba el pájaro," she'd say.
"Ven, Abuela. Come, Abuela," I'd say.
"Sí, quiero volar," Abuela would reply
as she leaped into the sky
with her skirt flapping in the wind.

We would fly all over the city.
"Mira," Abuela would say, pointing.

And I'd look, as we soared
over parks and streets, dogs and people.

We'd wave to the people waiting for the bus.
"Buenos días," we'd say.
"Buenos días. Good morning,"
they'd call up to us. We'd fly
over factories and trains . . .

and glide close to the sea.
"Cerca del mar," we'd say.
We'd almost touch the tops of waves.

Abuela's skirt would be a sail.
She could race with the sailboats.
I'll bet she'd win.

We'd fly to where the ships are docked,
and watch people unload fruits
from the land where Abuela grew up.
Mangos, bananas, papayas—
those are all Spanish words.
So are rodeo, patio, and burro.
Maybe we'd see a cousin of Abuela's
hooking boxes of fruit to a crane.
We saw her cousin Daniel once,
unloading and loading the ships.

Out past the boats in the harbor
we'd see the Statue of Liberty.
"Me gusta," Abuela would say.
Abuela really likes her.
I do too.

We would circle around Liberty's head
and wave to the people visiting her.
That would remind Abuela of when
she first came to this country.

"Vamos al aeropuerto," she'd say.
She'd take me to the airport where
the plane that first brought her landed.
"Cuidado," Abuela would tell me.
We'd have to be careful
as we went for a short ride.

Then we could fly to *tío* Pablo's
and *tía* Elisa's store.
Pablo is my uncle, my *tío*,
and Elisa is my aunt, my *tía*.
They'd be surprised when we flew in,
but they'd offer us a cool *limonada*.
Flying is hot work.
"Pero quiero volar más,"
Abuela would say.
She wants to fly more.
I want to fly more too.

We could fly to *las nubes*, the clouds.
One looks like a cat, *un gato*.
One looks like a bear, *un oso*.
One looks like a chair, *una silla*.
"Descansemos un momento,"
Abuela would say.
She wants to rest a moment.
We would rest in our chair,
and Abuela would hold me in her arms,
with the whole sky
our house, *nuestra casa*.

We'd be as high as airplanes,
balloons, and birds,
and higher than the tall buildings downtown.
But we'd fly there too
to look around.

We could find the building where my father works.
"Hola, papá," I'd say as I waved. And Abuela would
do a flip for fun as we passed by the windows.

"Mira," I hear Abuela say.
"Look," she's telling me.
I do look,
and we are back in the park.

We are walking by the lake.
Abuela probably wants to go for a boat ride.
"Vamos a otra aventura," she says.
She wants us to go for another adventure.
That's just one of the things I love
about Abuela.
She likes adventures.

Abuela takes my hand.
"*Vamos,*" she says.
"Let's go."

Think and Respond

1 What adventures do Rosalba and Abuela have in the city?

2 Why do you think the author uses Spanish words in the story?

3 How would this story be different if Rosalba and Abuela were walking instead of **swooping** through the air?

4 Would you like to travel with Rosalba and Abuela? Explain your answer.

5 How did looking for smaller words and word parts help you read long words that you didn't know?

Glossary

The capitalized syllable is stressed in pronunciation.

Abuela (ah-BWEH-lah) Grandmother

Buenos días (BWEH-nohs DEE-ahs) Good day

Cerca del mar (SEHR-kah dehl mahr) Close to the sea

Cuidado (kwee-DAH-doh) Be careful

Descansemos un momento (dehs-kahn-SEH-mohs oon moh-MEHN-toh) Let's rest a moment

El parque es lindo (ehl PAHR-kay ehs LEEN-doh) The park is beautiful

Hola, papá (OH-lah, pah-PAH) Hello, papa

Las nubes (lahs NOO-behs) The clouds

Limonada (lee-moh-NAH-dah) Lemonade

Me gusta (meh GOO-stah) I like

Mira (MEE-rah) Look

Nuestra casa (NWEH-strah CAH-sah) Our house

Pero quiero volar más (PEH-roh key-EH-roh boh-LAR mahs) But I would like to fly more

Rosalba el pájaro (roh-SAHL-bah ehl PAH-hah-roh) Rosalba the bird

Sí, quiero volar (see, kee-EH-roh boh-LAR) Yes, I want to fly

Tantos pájaros (TAHN-tohs PAH-hah-rohs) So many birds

Tía (TEE-ah) Aunt

Tío (TEE-oh) Uncle

Un gato (oon GAH-toh) A cat

Un oso (oon OH-soh) A bear

Una silla (OON-ah SEE-yah) A chair

Vamos (BAH-mohs) Let's go

Vamos al aeropuerto (BAH-mohs ahl ah-ehr-oh-PWEHR-toh) Let's go to the airport

Vamos a otra aventura (BAH-mohs ah OH-trah ah-behn-TOO-rah) Let's go on another adventure

Ven (behn) Come

Meet the Author
Arthur Dorros

Dear Readers,

"Abuela" is about my New York grandmother and about imagining flying. When I was in the second grade, I liked to fly kites. I watched my kite rise until it was just a tiny dot in the sky. I imagined what it would be like to soar in the sky like a bird.

Later, I could see much of New York City from the apartment building I lived in. The city appeared below, as it did for Rosalba and Abuela in the story. Imagine how your home might look from high above!

Your friend,

Arthur Dorros

Meet the Illustrator

Elisa Kleven

Visit *The Learning Site!*
www.harcourtschool.com

Dear Readers,

I enjoyed making the pictures for "Abuela." I did not know New York City very well, so Arthur Dorros drew a map to show me the places where Rosalba and Abuela would fly.

When I made the artwork for this story, I first drew pencil illustrations. Then I used pens, crayons, watercolors, and collage materials to finish the artwork. I even used some material from a blouse of mine to make Abuela's purse!

Your friend,

Elisa Kleven

Making Connections

Compare Texts

1 Why do you think "Abuela" is part of a theme called Travel Time?

2 Compare the setting of "Abuela" to the setting of another story you have read recently. How are the settings alike? How are they different?

3 Which parts of "Abuela" could happen in real life? Which parts could not happen?

Adventure in the Air

Imagine that you are flying around your own neighborhood like Rosalba and Abuela. Write a diary entry about your adventures.

> Tuesday
> Dear Diary,
>   Today I flew over my neighborhood! I saw my mom planting flowers in the backyard. I also saw my friends playing soccer.

Writing CONNECTION

All About Birds

S c i e n c e
CONNECTION

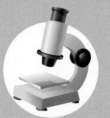

Find out more about the lives of birds. You can choose a bird from this list.

- robin
- sparrow
- eagle
- condor
- hummingbird

Write three facts about your bird. Then draw a picture of it.

Where Are You From?

Social Studies
CONNECTION

Rosalba's grandmother came to the United States from another country. Did members of your own family come from other countries? Find out where they lived before moving to this country. Show these places on a map. Share what you learn with classmates.

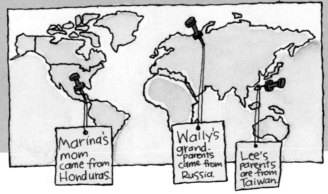

Marina's mom came from Honduras.

Wally's grandparents came from Russia.

Lee's parents are from Taiwan.

Words with *air* and *are*

Read these sentences from "Abuela."

We'd have to be <u>careful</u> as we went.
We would rest in our <u>chair</u>.

Say the underlined words *careful* and *chair*. Listen for the sound in each word. The letters **are** and **air** in a word stand for the same sound, even though they are spelled differently.

Here are some more words with that sound. Look for the letter patterns **air** and **are**. Say each word aloud. Which words have the same letter pattern?

fairy	**stare**	**repair**
barely	**hair**	**hare**
dare	**square**	**chairman**

Use these tips to read a longer word.
- Look for word parts you know.
- Break the word into parts.
- Say each part. Then blend the parts and say the word.

Test Prep

Words with are and air

Find the word that has the same sound as the underlined letters in the first word.

Example: st<u>air</u>

● square
○ store
○ car

Tip

Say each choice aloud. Be sure each word makes sense when you say it.

1. rep<u>air</u>

○ appear
○ cheer
○ hare

2. h<u>air</u>y

○ glare
○ heart
○ fear

Tip

On a real test, be sure to fill in the circle carefully.

3. prep<u>are</u>

○ unfair
○ opera
○ steer

Vocabulary Power

▲ Beginner's World Atlas

connects

distance

features

mapmaker

peel

This man is a **mapmaker**. His job is to make a flat picture of the round Earth.

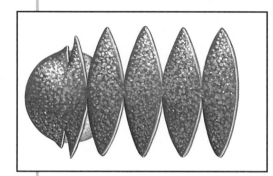 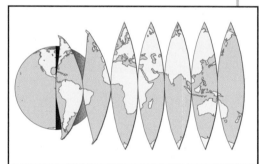

Find out how this works. First **peel** an orange in one piece. Then lay the orange piece flat. This is like a map of the Earth. The Earth is round like an orange. A map of the Earth is flat like an orange skin.

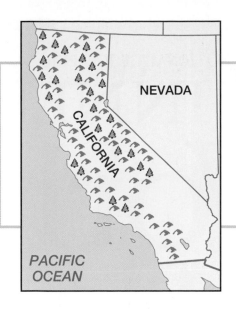

The mapmaker must show **features** of the land. The map will show deserts, forests, and mountains.

The mapmaker may also show cities on a map. If he **connects** two cities with a line, he can find out how far apart they are. He may write the **distance** beside the line to help travelers.

Vocabulary-Writing
CONNECTION

Make a list of other **features** that you might find on a map.

307

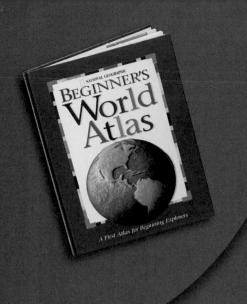

Nonfiction: Atlas

An atlas is a book of maps.

Look for

- map keys that help you understand the information on the maps.

- scales that tell you about distance.

NATIONAL GEOGRAPHIC

BEGINNER'S World Atlas

What Is a Map?

A map is a drawing of a place as it looks from above. It is flat, and it is smaller than the place it shows. A map can help you find where you are and where you want to go.

Mapping Your Backyard . . .

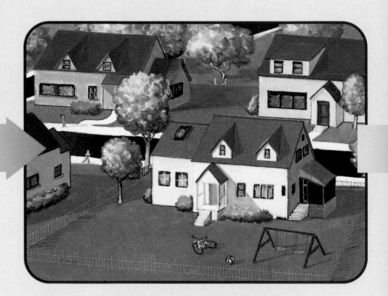

. . . from the ground

From your backyard you see everything in front of you straight on. You have to look up to see your roof and the tops of trees. You can't see what's in front of your house.

. . . from higher up

From higher up you look down on things. You can see the tops of trees and things in your yard and in the yards of other houses in your neighborhood.

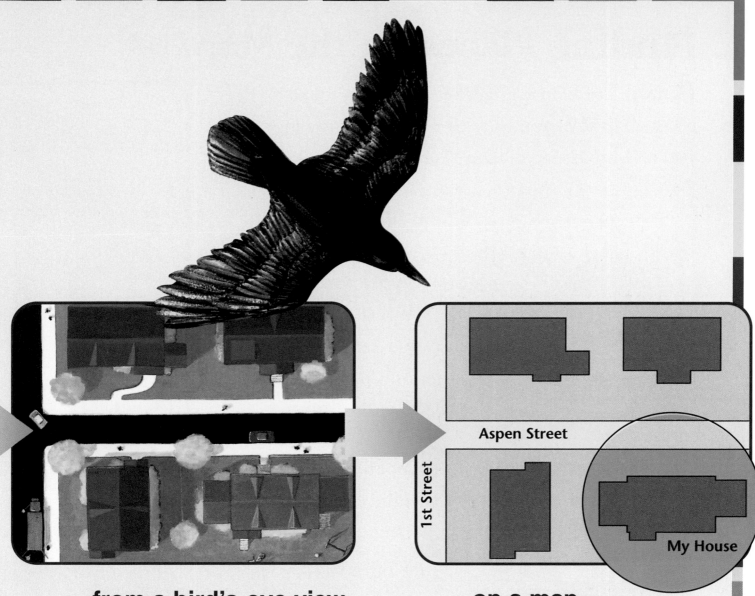

. . . from a bird's-eye view

If you were a bird flying directly overhead, you would only see the tops of things. You wouldn't see walls, tree trunks, tires, or feet.

. . . on a map

A map looks at places from a bird's-eye view, but it uses drawings called symbols to show things like houses that don't move.

Finding Places on the Map

A **map** can help you get where you want to
go. A map tells you how to read it by showing
you a compass, a key, and a scale.

◀ A **compass** helps you
travel in the right direction.
It tells you where north
(N), south (S), east (E), and
west (W) are on your map.
Sometimes it only shows
where north is.

▼ A **scale** tells you about distance on a map. Look
at the scale on the map at the right. The length of
the top bars is the same as traveling a hundred yards.

0	100 Yards

0	100 Meters

House
Store
School
Library
Play Area
Water

◀ A **map key** helps you understand
the symbols used by the mapmaker
to show things like houses, play
areas, and schools on the map.

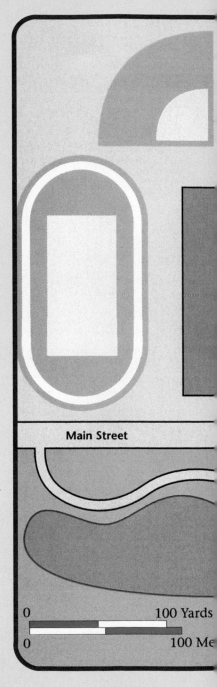

Main Street

0	100 Yards
0	100 Me

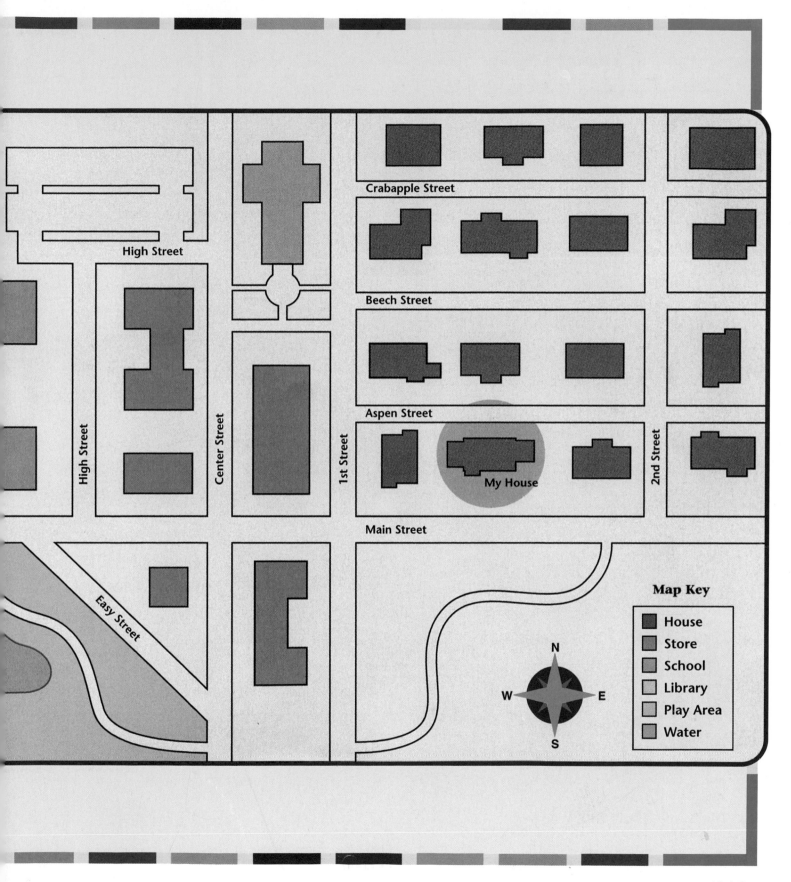

Making the Round Earth Flat

From your backyard the Earth probably looks flat. If you could travel into space like an astronaut, you would see that Earth is a giant ball with blue oceans, greenish-brown land, and white clouds. Even in space you can only see the part of Earth facing you. To see the whole Earth at one time you need a map. Maps take the round Earth and make it flat so you can see all of it at one time.

▶ Earth in Space

From space you can see that the Earth is round with oceans, land, and clouds. But you can see only half the Earth at one time.

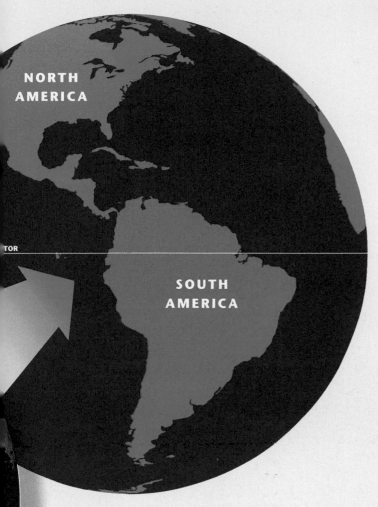

NORTH
AMERICA

TOR

SOUTH
AMERICA

▲ Earth as a Globe

A **globe** is a tiny model of the
Earth that you can put on a
stand or hold in your hand.
You have to turn it to see the
other side. You still can't see
the whole Earth at one time.

▼ Earth on Paper

If you could peel a globe like an
orange, you could make the Earth
flat, but there would be spaces
between the pieces. Mapmakers
stretch the land and the water at
the top and bottom to fill in the
spaces. This is how a **map** lets
you see the whole world all at
once.

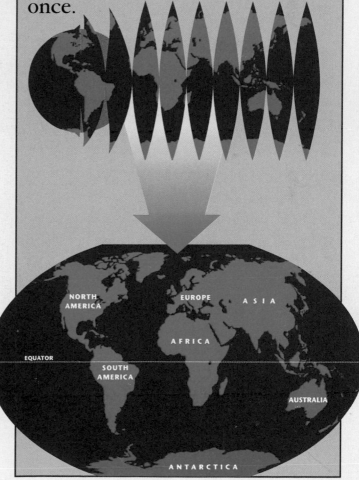

NORTH
AMERICA

EUROPE

ASIA

AFRICA

EQUATOR

SOUTH
AMERICA

AUSTRALIA

ANTARCTICA

The Physical World

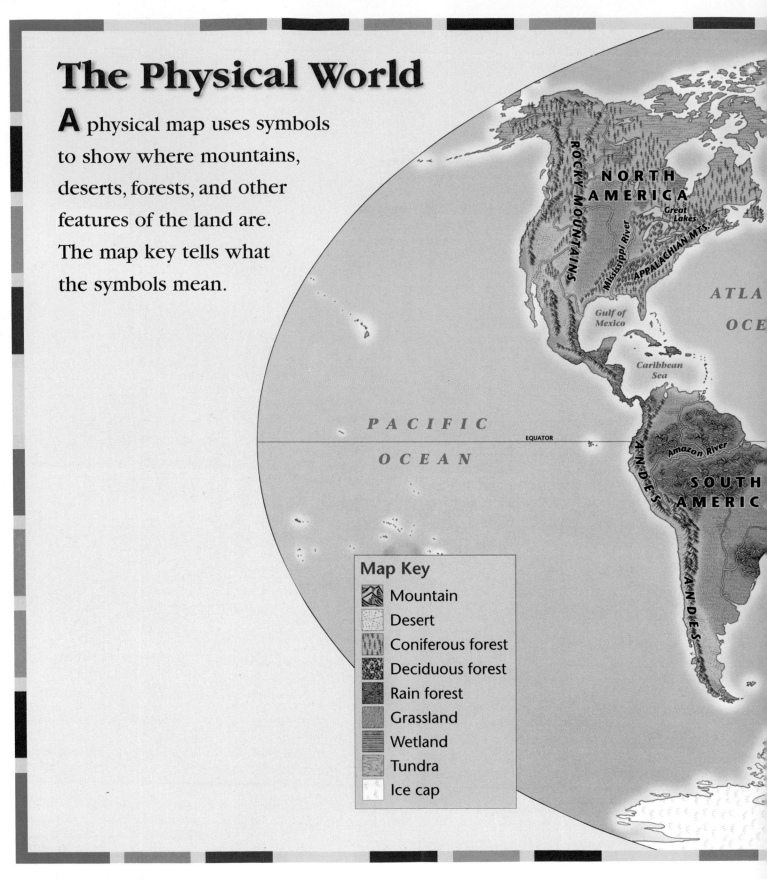

A physical map uses symbols to show where mountains, deserts, forests, and other features of the land are. The map key tells what the symbols mean.

NORTH AMERICA

ROCKY MOUNTAINS

Great Lakes

Mississippi River

APPALACHIAN MTS.

Gulf of Mexico

Caribbean Sea

ATLA
OCE

PACIFIC

OCEAN

EQUATOR

Amazon River

ANDES

SOUTH AMERIC

Map Key
- Mountain
- Desert
- Coniferous forest
- Deciduous forest
- Rain forest
- Grassland
- Wetland
- Tundra
- Ice cap

ARCTIC OCEAN

GREENLAND

EUROPE

ASIA

URAL Mts.

Volga River

Europe-Asia boundary

ALPS

Gobi

ATLAS MTS.

Mediterranean Sea

HIMALAYA

Yangtze River

SAHARA

AFRICA

Nile River

PACIFIC OCEAN

EQUATOR

INDIAN OCEAN

AUSTRALIA

GREAT DIVIDING RANGE

ANTARCTICA

The Physical World Close Up

The Earth's surface is made up of land and water. The biggest landmasses are called **continents.** All seven of them are named on this map. **Islands** are smaller pieces of land that are surrounded by water. Greenland is the largest island. Land that is nearly surrounded by water is called a **peninsula.** Europe has lots of them.

Oceans are the largest bodies of water. Can you find all four oceans? **Lakes** are bodies of water surrounded by land—like the Great Lakes, in North America. A large stream of water that flows into a lake or an ocean is called a **river.** The Nile is Earth's longest river.

ARCT

GREENLAND

NORTH AMERICA

ROCKY MOUNTAINS

Great Lakes

Mississippi River

APPALACHIAN MTS.

ATLANTIC OCEAN

Gulf of Mexico

Caribbean Sea

PACIFIC OCEAN

EQUATOR

Amazon River

ANDES

SOUTH AMERICA

ANDES

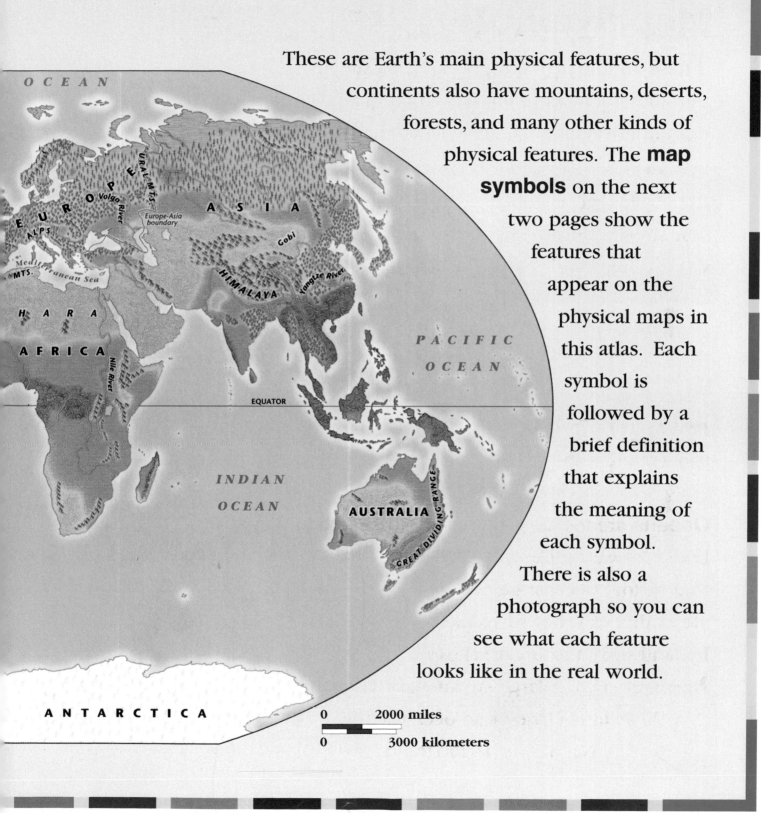

These are Earth's main physical features, but continents also have mountains, deserts, forests, and many other kinds of physical features. The **map symbols** on the next two pages show the features that appear on the physical maps in this atlas. Each symbol is followed by a brief definition that explains the meaning of each symbol. There is also a photograph so you can see what each feature looks like in the real world.

OCEAN

EUROPE

URAL MTS.

Volga River

Europe-Asia boundary

ASIA

ALPS

Gobi

Mediterranean Sea

MTS.

HIMALAYA

Yangtze River

HARA

PACIFIC OCEAN

AFRICA

Nile River

EQUATOR

INDIAN OCEAN

AUSTRALIA

GREAT DIVIDING RANGE

ANTARCTICA

0   2000 miles

0   3000 kilometers

Map Symbols

These are the map symbols used on the physical maps in this atlas. Each continent has different kinds of features, so each physical map will have its own map key.

 Mountain

Land that rises at least 1,000 feet above the surrounding land

 Desert

Very dry land that can be hot or cold and sandy or rocky

 Coniferous forest

Forest with trees that have seed cones and often needlelike leaves

 Deciduous forest

Forest with trees that lose leaves in fall and grow new ones in spring

 Rain forest

Forest with trees that keep their leaves all year and need lots of rain

 Ice cap

A permanent sheet of thick ice that covers the land, as in Antarctica

 Tundra

A cold region with low plants that grow during warm months

 Wetland

Land, such as a marsh or swamp, that is mostly covered with water

 Grassland

A grass-covered area with too little rain for many trees to grow

321

North America

North America is shaped like a triangle ▼. It is wide in the north. In the south it narrows to a strip of land so narrow that a Marathon runner could cross it in two hours. Ships make the trip on the Panama Canal. The warm islands in the Caribbean Sea are part of North America. So is icy Greenland in the far north. The seven countries between Mexico and South America make up a region commonly called Central America. It connects the rest of North America and South America.

Kha-hay! I'm from the Crow tribe in Montana. This beautiful valley is in Yosemite National Park, in California. It's in the Sierra Nevada mountains. Look for them on the map when you turn the next page.

322

North America

The Land

Land regions The Rocky Mountains run along the west side of North America through Mexico. There, the mountains are called the Sierra Madre Oriental. Lower mountains called the Appalachians are in the east. Grassy plains lie between the two mountain chains.

Water The longest rivers are the Mississippi and the Missouri. The Great Lakes are the world's largest group of freshwater lakes.

Climate The far north is icy cold. Temperatures get warmer as you move south. Much of Central America is hot and wet.

Plants North America has large forests where there is plenty of rain. Grasslands cover drier areas.

Animals There is a big variety of animals—everything from bears, moose, and wolves to monkeys and colorful parrots.

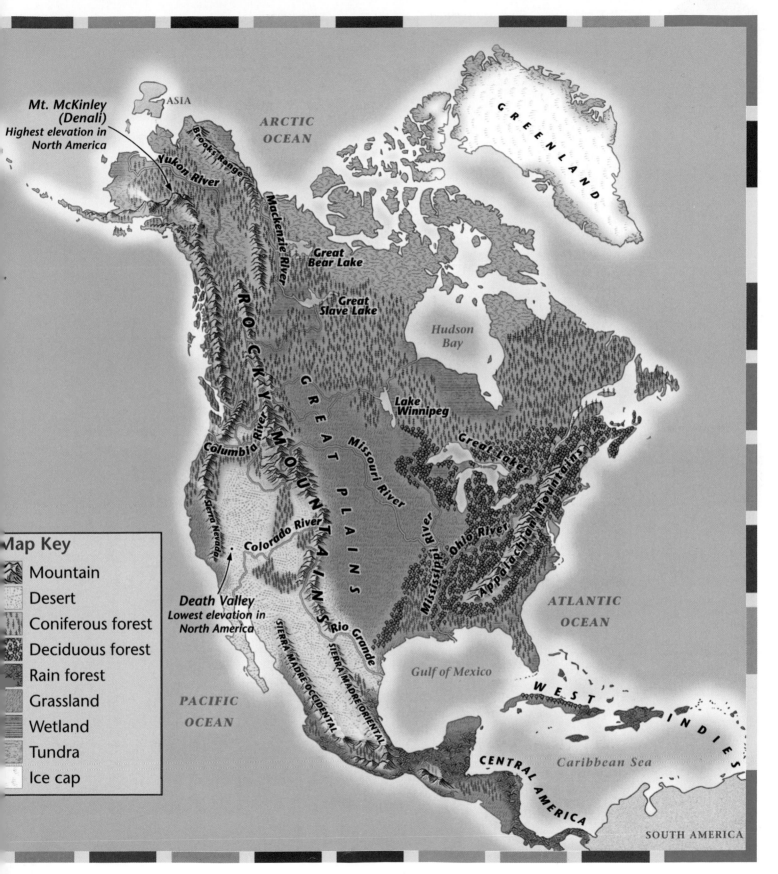

Mt. McKinley
(Denali)
Highest elevation in
North America

ASIA

ARCTIC
OCEAN

GREENLAND

Brooks Range

Yukon River

Mackenzie River

Great
Bear Lake

Great
Slave Lake

Hudson
Bay

R O C K Y   M O U N T A I N S

Columbia River

Sierra Nevada

Colorado River

Death Valley
Lowest elevation in
North America

G R E A T   P L A I N S

Missouri River

Lake
Winnipeg

Great Lakes

Mississippi River

Ohio River

Appalachian Mountains

ATLANTIC
OCEAN

Rio Grande

SIERRA MADRE OCCIDENTAL

SIERRA MADRE ORIENTAL

Gulf of Mexico

PACIFIC
OCEAN

W E S T

I N D I E S

Caribbean Sea

CENTRAL AMERICA

SOUTH AMERICA

Map Key
- Mountain
- Desert
- Coniferous forest
- Deciduous forest
- Rain forest
- Grassland
- Wetland
- Tundra
- Ice cap

325

North America

▼ Palm trees grow along sandy beaches on islands in the **Caribbean Sea.** In this part of North America the weather is warm year-round.

▲ North America is famous for its **deciduous forests.** Leaves turn fiery colors each fall!

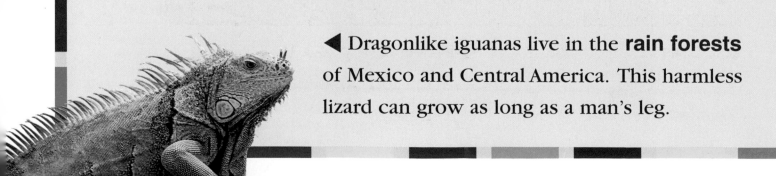

◄ Dragonlike iguanas live in the **rain forests** of Mexico and Central America. This harmless lizard can grow as long as a man's leg.

▶ This view from a plane shows that **Greenland** has high mountains and lots of snow and ice.

◀ A white-tail deer nuzzles her babies in a meadow near the **Great Lakes.** Deer live in almost every country on the continent.

▲ **Deserts** are found in the southwestern part of North America. The large rock formation on the right is called The Mitten. Can you guess why?

North America

The People

Countries Canada, the United States, Mexico, and the countries of Central America and the West Indies make up North America.

Cities Mexico City is the biggest city in North America. Next in size are New York City and Los Angeles. Havana, in Cuba, is the largest city in the West Indies.

People The ancestors of most people in North America came from Europe. Many other people trace their roots to Africa and Asia. Native Americans live throughout.

Languages English and Spanish are the main languages. A large number of people in Canada and Haiti speak French. There are also many Native American languages.

Products North America's chief products include cars, machinery, petroleum, natural gas, silver, wheat, corn, beef, and forest products.

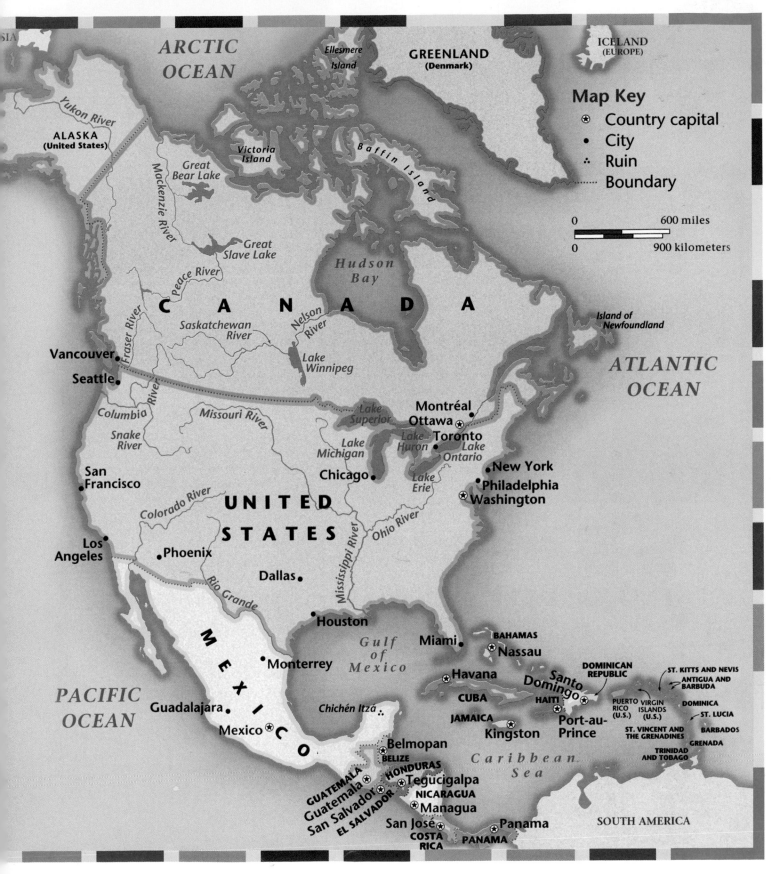

ARCTIC
OCEAN

Ellesmere Island

GREENLAND
(Denmark)

ICELAND
(EUROPE)

Map Key
⊛ Country capital
● City
∴ Ruin
⋯⋯ Boundary

Yukon River

ALASKA
(United States)

Victoria Island

Great Bear Lake

Baffin Island

0   600 miles

0   900 kilometers

Mackenzie River

Great Slave Lake

Peace River

Fraser River

C A N A D A

Saskatchewan River

Nelson River

Hudson Bay

Island of Newfoundland

ATLANTIC
OCEAN

Vancouver ●

Seattle ●

Columbia River

Lake Winnipeg

Snake River

Missouri River

San
Francisco ●

Colorado River

U N I T E D
S T A T E S

Lake Superior

Montréal ●
Ottawa ⊛
Lake Huron Toronto ●
Lake Michigan *Lake Ontario*

Chicago ●

Lake Erie

New York ●
Philadelphia ●
⊛ Washington

Los
Angeles ●

Phoenix ●

Ohio River

Dallas ●

Rio Grande

Mississippi River

Houston ●

M E X I C O

*Gulf
of
Mexico*

Miami ●

BAHAMAS
⊛ Nassau

DOMINICAN
REPUBLIC

ST. KITTS AND NEVIS
ANTIGUA AND
BARBUDA

PACIFIC
OCEAN

Monterrey ●

Guadalajara ●

Chichén Itzá ∴

⊛ Havana

CUBA

Santo
Domingo

HAITI

PUERTO VIRGIN
RICO ISLANDS
(U.S.) (U.S.)

DOMINICA

ST. LUCIA

Mexico ⊛

Belmopan ⊛
BELIZE

JAMAICA

Kingston ⊛

Port-au-
Prince ⊛

BARBADOS

ST. VINCENT AND
THE GRENADINES

GRENADA

GUATEMALA
Guatemala ⊛
San Salvador ⊛
EL SALVADOR

HONDURAS
Tegucigalpa ●
NICARAGUA
⊛ Managua

*Caribbean
Sea*

TRINIDAD
AND TOBAGO

San José ⊛
COSTA
RICA

PANAMA

⊛ Panama

SOUTH AMERICA

North America

▶ Skiing and ski jumping are popular sports in the **Rocky Mountains.**

◀ This is **Mexico City.** More people live here than in any other city in North America.

▶ These red berries hold coffee beans. Many farmers in **Guatemala** make a living growing coffee.

◀ This pyramid at **Chichén Itzá** was built long ago by the Maya people.

◀ This boy is dressed like a jaguar for a celebration in **Mexico.** Many people admire the jaguar for its strength and courage.

◀ This farmer is harvesting wheat on a big farm in **Canada.** Canada and the United States grow much of the world's wheat.

▶ Ships travel across Panama on the Panama Canal. It is a shortcut between the Atlantic and the Pacific Oceans.

Think and Respond

1 What information do the maps and photographs in this selection give you?

2 How does a map key help you read a map?

3 Which map would you use to show where the biggest rivers of North America are located? Why?

4 If you drew a map of your school, what **features** would you include?

5 What strategies did you use to read longer words in this selection?

Making Connections

Compare Texts

1   Why do you think this selection is part of a theme called Travel Time?

2   How are the maps of North America on pages 325 and 329 different? In what ways are they alike?

3   How did the photographs in "Beginner's World Atlas" help you better understand the map information?

Make a Glossary

Make a glossary of map words. First reread the selection. Find five words in **bold** type. Then write each word and what it means.

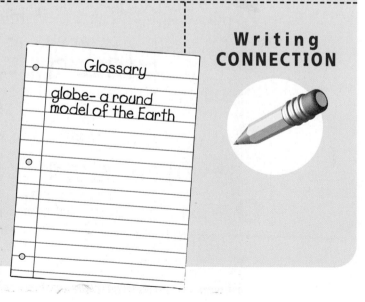

Glossary

globe- a round model of the Earth

Writing CONNECTION

Map a Room

Make a map of your classroom. On your map, show where the furniture is placed. Make a map key. Then write a title and share your map with classmates.

Key:
- teacher's desk
- desk
- table
- chair

Mrs. Green's Classroom

Make a Graph

Draw a map of your neighborhood. Then make a picture graph to show how many houses are on each street. Make a key for your picture graph.

My Neighborhood

Front Street
Curtis Lane
Windy Hill
Back Row

Key: Each □ = 1 house

Locate Information

You can use a **table of contents** at the beginning of a book to help you find information. Many tables of contents list **chapters** in a book and the page number for the start of each chapter.

Look at this table of contents. What kinds of information does it show?

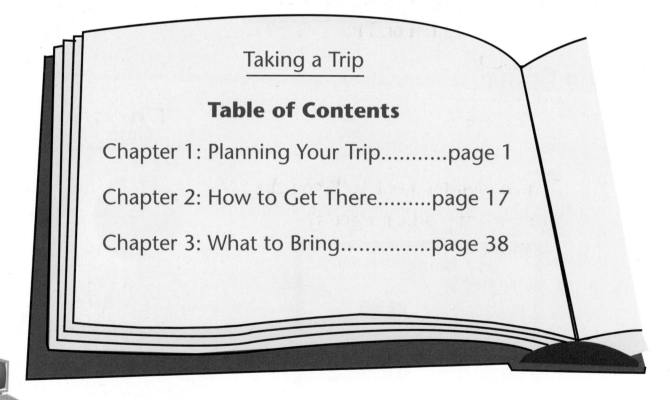

Taking a Trip

Table of Contents

Visit *The Learning Site!*
www.harcourtschool.com

See *Skills* and *Activities*

Read the table of contents. Then answer the questions below it.

The Perfect Bike
Table of Contents

---

1. **On which page would you begin to find information on bike safety?**

    ○ page 1

    ○ page 15

    ○ page 27

Tip

Use your finger to guide you as you read.

2. **Which chapter would tell you the most about a bike's wheels?**

    ○ Chapter 1

    ○ Chapter 2

    ○ Chapter 3

Tip

Read each chapter title. Think about the information you might find in each chapter.

▲ Dinosaurs Travel

Vocabulary Power

cassette

companions

luggage

relatives

sturdy

Hello! I am Amanda, and this is a picture of me with Mom and Dad. They were my **companions** on an airplane trip.

We visited Uncle Danny, Aunt Rose, and some other **relatives**.

Before we went to the airport, I packed my clothes in a strong, **sturdy** suitcase. My mom and dad packed their **luggage**, too.

We took along presents for Uncle Danny's birthday. I gave him a card. Dad and Mom gave him a **cassette** of his favorite music.

Vocabulary-Writing CONNECTION

Write a short description of a trip you have taken. Tell who your **companions** were and what you packed in your **luggage**.

Genre

Nonfiction: Informational Book

An informational book gives information about a topic.

Look for

- headings that tell you what a page is about.

- facts that are presented in a way that makes sense.

Laurie Krasny Brown
and
Marc Brown

Traveling

Do you ever wish you could climb a mountain,

fly through the air,

or ride around town in a long limousine?

Every time you leave home,
whether to travel

around the world,

or around the block,
get ready for an adventure!

Getting Ready for a Trip

Books and maps can help you learn about a new place before you go there.

You may not be able to take your pets with you, but someone else will take good care of them.

If you take the addresses of friends and relatives, you can write to them while you're away.

Find out about the weather where you're going and choose clothes that will be good to wear. Only pack a few toys, games, books, and tapes. Small, light, and sturdy things travel best.

Remember one or two favorite companions.

And don't forget these!

Getting From Place to Place

Wherever you're headed, getting there can be part of the fun!

On Foot

Walking lets you stop
and see the sights.

You may meet other travelers
along the way.

You can hike on a trail where
almost no one ever goes.

And your body is all that
you need!

Your Own Wheels

Bicycles and skateboards are faster than walking. You're the driver! It's up to you to know the rules of the road.

Keep your bike or board in good working order, so you're all set to ride anytime.

With your own set of wheels, you can go most anywhere!

You and your family can go biking together.

Sometimes you have to pedal hard to get where you're going,

but downhill you get a free ride!

347

By Car

Cars will take you on all kinds of roads. Riding on the highways is fastest!

Driving on back roads is slower but you see more.

You and your family can go wherever or whenever you want. You can bring along lots of your things— if you have room!

You and your family can play word games while you ride. You can take turns reading road signs or looking at different license plates.

It feels good to get out and stretch your legs from time to time.

Switching seats will give you different views.

If you have a cassette player, you can bring your favorite tapes.

Riding the Subway and Bus

In some cities riding underground in a subway is the fastest way to travel.

On a bus you can see what's going on outside. A tour bus driver will point out the sights.

On a subway or bus you must pay a fare to ride.

Subways and buses make many stops. Don't forget to watch for yours!

Taking the Train

You can buy a ticket for the train at the station. Look at the signs for your track and departure time. All aboard! Taking the train is a great way to see new places!

On most trains, you can sit facing forward or backward. The conductor announces each stop the train makes. You can follow along with a timetable.

Trains don't have to stop until they pull into a station. The train stops at many stations so passengers can get on and off.

351

Flying in Planes

At the airport an agent looks at your ticket, checks your luggage, and assigns you a seat on the plane.

Airport security makes sure no one carries anything dangerous or illegal on the plane.

You can bring a small bag on most planes and stow it under or above your seat. Buckle up!

Take off!

As the plane climbs higher, things below look smaller and smaller.

You'll fly up above the clouds!

Coming Home

When it's time to go home, remember to pack all your things. You may want to bring back a gift for someone special. Souvenirs and pictures will remind you of your trip.

At home, things may look different to you.

It's fun to go home again and see friends and relatives.

You can play with all your toys, eat your favorite snacks, and dream about where to travel next!

Think and Respond

1 What are some important things to remember before and as you travel?

2 How can the headings help you understand and summarize "Dinosaurs Travel"?

3 If the Browns asked you to add a travel tip to this book, what would you write?

4 Where would you go for an adventure? Who would your **companions** be?

5 What strategy did you use to figure out the meaning of a word that you didn't know?

Meet the Author

Laurie Krasny Brown

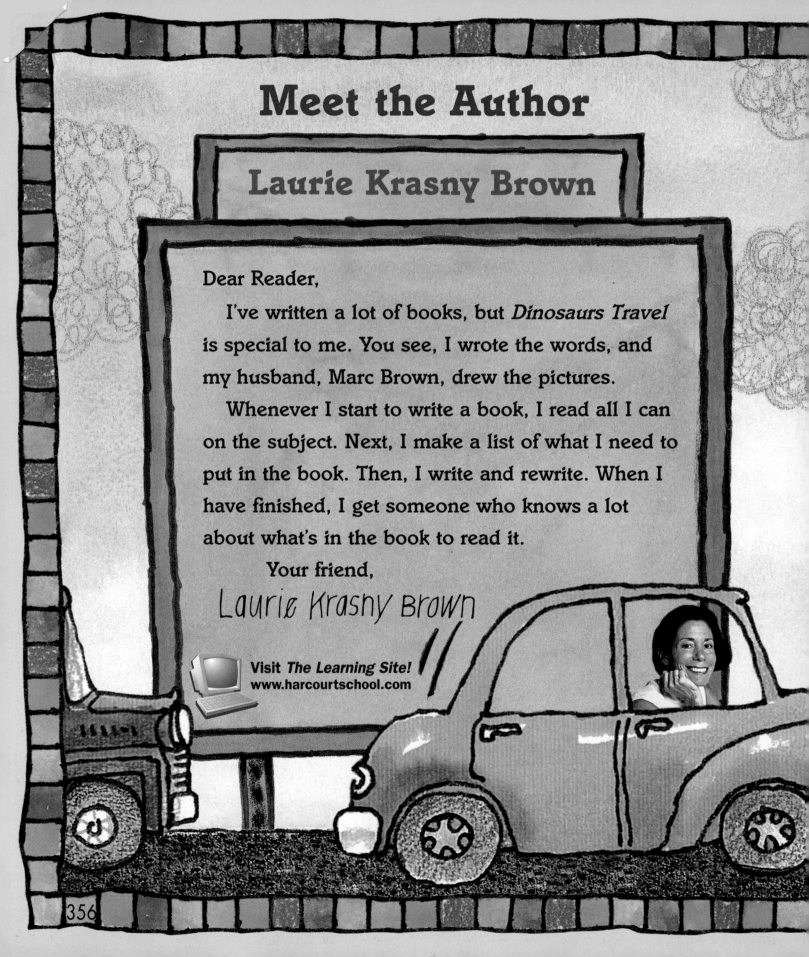

Dear Reader,

I've written a lot of books, but *Dinosaurs Travel* is special to me. You see, I wrote the words, and my husband, Marc Brown, drew the pictures.

Whenever I start to write a book, I read all I can on the subject. Next, I make a list of what I need to put in the book. Then, I write and rewrite. When I have finished, I get someone who knows a lot about what's in the book to read it.

Your friend,

Laurie Krasny Brown

Visit *The Learning Site!*
www.harcourtschool.com

Meet the Illustrator

Marc Brown

Dear Reader,

Many kids know my artwork from my Arthur books, but I like to do information books, too. I have done several books using these dinosaur characters. I chose to draw dinosaurs because they are powerful animals, and I want my readers to feel powerful. I am proud of these books because I think they help kids feel good about themselves.

When I am not working, I like to spend time gardening. My wife, Laurie, and I grow flowers, fruits, and vegetables.

Your friend,

Marc Brown

KEEPING A ROAD JOURNAL

by Joy Beck • illustrated by Patti H. Goodnow

Road trips are a lot of fun, especially when you keep track of the interesting things you see and do, the neat people you meet, and all the new things you learn. Here's how:

You need:

- A new notebook
  (Spiral-bound notebooks work best.)
- A supply of sharpened pencils
- Adhesive tape
- An inexpensive, disposable camera

Directions:

1. On the first page, print your name, age, date of the trip, and your traveling pals.

2. Turn the page. On the left page, write: "Date," "Time," "Location," and "Weather." On the right page, write: "What Happened Today." These two pages are for the *first* day of the trip.

3. Prepare the next two pages the same way for the *second* day.

4. Prepare enough pages in your journal for the whole trip. (If you do enough in advance, you'll be more likely to actually fill them in later.)

Going on the Record

Gather material for your journal by answering these questions each day:

- Where did we go?
- What did we see?
- What did we do?
- Who did we meet?
- How was all this different from home?

Remember to interview your family. Did they like the same things as you?

Take plenty of pictures, too. Then make a note in your journal so you'll know what they were about and why you took them.

Making Connections

Compare Texts

1　Why do you think "Beginner's World Atlas" comes before "Dinosaurs Travel" in this theme?

2　Think about the pictures in "Dinosaurs Travel" and "Beginner's World Atlas." How do they help you understand the selections?

3　How is the writing in "Dinosaurs Travel" like the writing in "Keeping a Road Journal"?

Invitation to Travel

Think of someone you would like to invite for a visit to your home. Write a short letter to invite that person. Remember to include all the parts of a letter.

Writing CONNECTION

Dinosaur Details

Find out about actual dinosaurs that lived long ago. Do research to learn about one of these dinosaurs:

- apatosaurus
- stegosaurus
- triceratops
- tyrannosaurus rex

Then make a "Dinosaur Details" poster. Draw pictures of your dinosaur and write facts about it. Tell how your dinosaur was different from other dinosaurs.

Great Escapes

There are many amazing places to visit on Earth. Look on a map to find each of these amazing places:

- Mount Everest
- the Nile River
- the Great Lakes
- the Grand Canyon

Then talk with classmates about what you learned. Name the continent where you would find each.

Words with ou and ough

Read this sentence from "Dinosaurs Travel."

Do you ever wish you could climb a mountain or fly through the air?

Say the underlined words, *you* and *through*. These words have the same vowel sound. The letters **ou** and **ough** stand for that vowel sound.

Look for the letter patterns **ou** and **ough** in the next two words. Say each aloud.

gr<u>ou</u>p   thr<u>ough</u>

Now read the following words. Point to the letters that stand for the vowel sound in **you**.

you'd   grouping   throughout   soup

> **Use these tips to read a longer word.**
> * Look for word parts you know.
> * Break the word into parts.
> * Say each part. Then blend the parts and say the word.

Test Prep

Words with *ou* and *ough*

GEORGIA
CRCT Tested Skill

Find the word that has the same sound as the underlined letters in the first word.

Example: **thr<u>ough</u>**
- ○ below
- ● you
- ○ throw

Tip

Look at the underlined letters closely. Be sure you know the sound they make.

1. **gr<u>ou</u>p**
   - ○ grape
   - ○ soup
   - ○ steep

2. **y<u>ou</u>**
   - ○ stop
   - ○ look
   - ○ throughout

Tip

Skip choices that don't make sense.

3. **y<u>ou</u>'ve**
   - ○ trot
   - ○ regroup
   - ○ yarn

▲ Montigue on the
High Seas

Vocabulary Power

cozy

drifted

fleet

launched

looming

realized

It was a cool day, but Juan and his brother felt warm and **cozy** in their jackets. The tall trees were **looming** above them.

Juan and José made paper boats. Soon they had a whole **fleet** of them.

The boys **launched** the boats by pushing them out into the water. The boats **drifted** slowly with the breeze across the pond.

Juan looked at his watch. He **realized** it was time to go. "Come on, José," he said to his brother. "It's almost dinnertime!"

Vocabulary-Writing CONNECTION

Think of something that makes you feel warm and **cozy**. Write a short description of it.

Genre

Story

A story has characters, a setting, and a plot.

Look for

- a problem that characters solve by the end of the story.

- pictures that help tell the story.

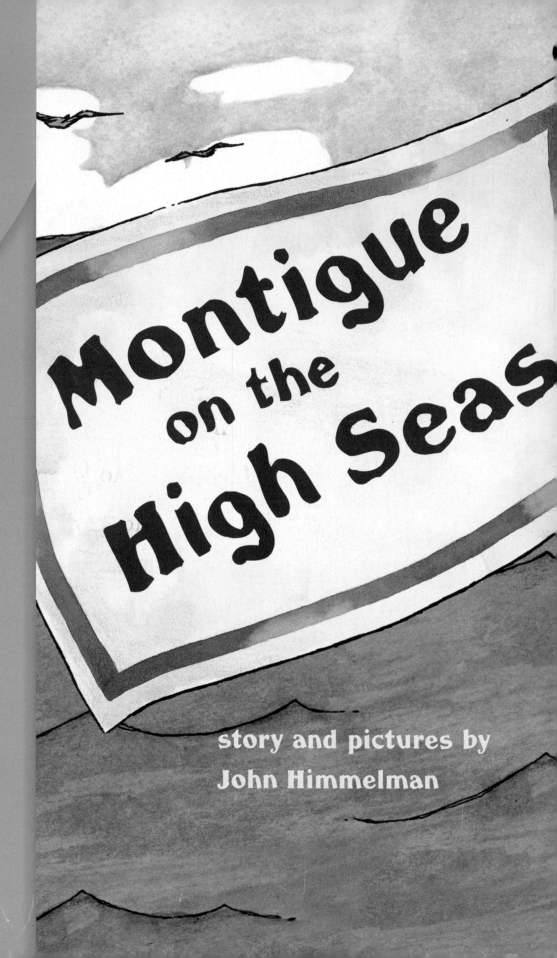

Montigue on the High Seas

story and pictures by
John Himmelman

In a cozy hole by the sea, there lived a young mole. His name was Montigue. Montigue loved his home. It was cool in the afternoons and warm in the evenings.

One day it began to rain. Soon the rain was coming down in buckets. By evening, Montigue's home was flooded. He had to find a safe place to spend the night. Montigue swam and swam until at last he noticed a funny-looking house propped on a rock. He was so tired that he fell into a deep sleep as soon as he crawled inside.

Montigue woke up rested and warm. It was a few moments before he realized that he had been . . .

. . . swept out to sea!

Poor Montigue drifted for days with nothing to drink except lime soda and nothing to eat but seaweed.

He grew lonely and bored as he stared at the horizon day after day. Then one morning, he noticed a dark shadow beneath him. Suddenly, he was thrown into the air by a giant humpback whale! Montigue clung to the bottle as it slowly filled with water and sank.

371

A passing fish, spotting an interesting meal, swallowed the bottle, mole and all! Before Montigue knew what was happening, the fish was yanked  up by a huge net. Montigue and the bottle fell out of its mouth and onto the deck of a ship.

Montigue looked up half-dazed and saw a giant sailor looming over him. He was holding a giant cat! The cat leapt after him, but Montigue  scuttled into a hole. "Safe at last," he thought.

"What a funny-looking mouse," said a voice beside him.

Montigue was surrounded by mice. "What were you doing out there?" asked one, nervously. "Don't you know that Barnacles the Cat is trying to clear us all off this ship?"

Montigue began to tell them how he came to the ship. He told of battling raging seas, riding giant whales, fighting off mole-eating fish, and he told them of the crash of his bottle ship. Just as he was coming to the end of his story, Montigue fell off his perch and knocked over a box of kitchen supplies.

When things settled down, the mice cheered. Montigue had given them an idea. The mice scurried in every direction, collecting bits of cloth, rags, and other supplies. Even Montigue got caught up in the fun.

They all worked together and soon their fleet was launched. The mice elected Montigue their captain. As they glided over the sea, he began to enjoy the thrill of guiding the ships through the waves. In a few days, one of the mice shouted, "LAND HO!"

When they were safely ashore, the mice carried Montigue on their shoulders. They asked him to live with them and he happily accepted. They started building their homes right away.

Montigue loved his new home. It was cool in the afternoons and warm in the evenings. And now he had lots of friendly neighbors.

And if he ever felt the pull of the high seas, he still had his bottle and his sail.

Think and Respond

❶ What happened to Montigue after he **drifted** onto the high seas?

❷ Why is the setting important to this story?

❸ Why do you think the author has Montigue meet the mice on the ship?

❹ What part of Montigue's adventure do you like the best?

❺ What strategies did you use to help you read this story?

John Himmelman

John Himmelman gets the ideas for his stories from the pictures he draws of characters like Montigue. The pictures help him to decide what a character will do in a story. "A story is just a story, but the characters become very real to me," he says. When he's not creating children's books, John Himmelman likes to play the guitar.

379

Making Connections

Compare Texts

1 Why do you think "Montigue on the High Seas" is in the same theme as "Abuela"?

2 Think about the setting at the beginning of the story and at the end. How are the settings alike? How are they different?

3 If Montigue decides to travel on the high seas again, what parts of "Dinosaurs Travel" do you think he should read? Why?

Write a Letter

May 19, 2003

Dear Harold,

You will never believe what happened to me!

Imagine that you are Montigue. Write a short letter to a friend, telling about your adventures. Be sure to include the important details.

Writing CONNECTION

Bottle Music

Fill five bottles with different amounts of water. Tap each bottle gently with a pencil and listen for how high or low the sound is—its *pitch*. Put the bottles in order from highest to lowest pitch. What makes the pitch high or low?

Find the High Seas

Look at a world map, and find the names of all four oceans. Write them down. Now look for the names of the three oceans that touch North America. Circle them on your list.

Homophones

Homophones are words that sound the same but are spelled differently. They also have different meanings.

I'm eating
a **pear**.

That's a nice
pair of shoes.

The tree is
bare in winter.

The **bear** likes
to eat honey.

He **ate** the
cookie.

I have **eight**
cookies.

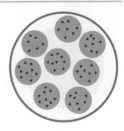

Can you complete this sentence with the correct word?

right   write

She will _____ a letter.

Test Prep
Homophones

Choose the correct word to complete each sentence.

1. It will take an _____ for us to drive home.
   - ○ our
   - ○ hour

2. At _____, the moon was high in the sky.
   - ○ knight
   - ○ night

3. I put the book over _____, on the table.
   - ○ there
   - ○ they're

Tip

Try to picture the right answer in your mind.

4. That dog has a very short _____ .
   - ○ tale
   - ○ tail

383

Vocabulary Power

feat

heroine

hospitality

refused

spectators

stood

Hi! I'm Dana. I went with my family to see an air show.

With other **spectators**, we watched a pilot fly upside down. That was an amazing **feat**! One pilot held a flying record that **stood** for three years.

I bought a picture of Amelia Earhart. She was a flying **heroine**. She was the first woman to fly across the Atlantic Ocean alone!

My brother **refused** to leave at the end of the show. He didn't want to go home.

On the way home, we stopped at my aunt's house. She gave us milk and cookies. We thanked her for her **hospitality**.

Vocabulary–Writing CONNECTION

Think about a time when you did something no one thought you could do. Write a paragraph to tell about your amazing **feat**.

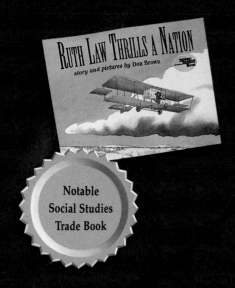

Notable
Social Studies
Trade Book

Genre

Nonfiction: Biography

A biography is the story of a person's life.

Look for

- events in time order.

- information telling why the person's life is important.

RUTH LAW

story and pictures
by Don Brown

THRILLS A NATION

On November 19, 1916, Ruth Law tried to fly from Chicago to New York City in one day.

It had never been done before.

It was a frosty, blustery morning. Ruth woke up before dawn, but she did not feel the cold. To get used to the cold weather, she had slept in a tent on the roof of a Chicago hotel.

She put on two woolen suits, one on top of the other.

Then she put on two leather suits and covered her bulky outfit with a skirt.

In 1916, a polite lady *always* wore a skirt.

It was still dark when Ruth went to Grant Park on the Lake Michigan shore, where her plane was waiting. It was the tiny one she flew in air shows. Ruth called it a baby machine. It was good for stunts like loop-the-loop, but it was small and old. Ruth had tried to buy a newer, bigger plane for her long flight, but Mr. Curtiss, the manufacturer, had refused to sell her one. Hundreds of pilots had already been injured or killed flying, and Mr. Curtiss did not believe a woman could fly a large plane.

Mechanics had worked all night on the plane. They had attached a special windshield to protect Ruth from the cold wind, and had added a second gas tank so she would not have to stop for fuel more than once. Now the plane could carry fifty-three gallons of gasoline. But the additional gasoline made the plane too heavy. To get rid of some extra weight, the mechanics took the lights off the plane. Without them, Ruth would have to reach New York City before nightfall.

The freezing weather made the engine hard to start. More than an hour passed before Ruth could get under way.

At 7:20 A.M., Ruth climbed into the cockpit. She removed her skirt and stuffed it behind her seat—good sense defeated fashion.

She opened the throttle. The plane leaped forward and bounced over bumps and hollows. It raced awkwardly across the ground, then lifted toward the sky.

A fierce wind whipped through Chicago. It shook and tossed the small plane.

A dozen onlookers watched in fear.

A mechanic cried.

Ruth struggled to steady the plane as it dipped and pitched in the wind.

She narrowly topped the buildings and slowly climbed into the sky above Chicago. Ruth Law was on her way to New York City.

A mile above ground, Ruth sliced through the frigid winter air at one hundred miles an hour. She set her course by consulting the crude scroll of maps she had taped together and attached to her leg. She also had a compass, a clock, and a speedometer.

Ruth flew for nearly six hours. She was depending on the wind to help carry her from Chicago to New York City. But the wind died down. Only gasoline propelled the plane.

At approximately 2:00 P.M. eastern standard time, she neared
Hornell, New York, where a group of supporters was waiting.

Then the engine quit.

The fuel tank was empty and Hornell was still two miles away.

The plane pitched slightly and sank. Ruth had only one
chance to make a safe landing.

She struggled to control the steering gear. The field seemed to come up at her. The crowd of spectators spilled into her path. The plane brushed their heads.

Ruth was on the ground.

She was so cold and hungry that she had to be helped to a nearby car. She was driven to a restaurant for a lunch of scrambled eggs and coffee while her plane was refueled.

She had flown 590 miles nonstop. It was a record. No one in America had ever flown farther.

But Ruth's flight was not over.

At 3:24 P.M., Ruth set out again for New York City.

All day, newspapers told the story of Ruth's flight. A crowd in Binghamton, New York, had turned out, hoping to see her fly overhead. They were not disappointed. At first she was just a speck in the sky, but soon she made a striking cameo against the late afternoon sun.

Suddenly the plane slanted toward the ground and disappeared behind some trees.

"She's down! Something's broken!"

Nothing was broken. Ruth had decided to land. New York
City was two hours away, but she would not be able to read her
instruments in the dark. She tied the plane to a tree, wrapped
her skirt around her, and accepted the hospitality of strangers.

The next morning, Ruth flew to New York City.

When she landed, an army general and a military band were there to greet her. Ruth was a heroine. "You beat them all!" the general said as he shook her hand.

Newspapers heralded her feat.

President Woodrow Wilson called her great.

A huge banquet was given in her honor.

On November 19, 1916, Ruth Law tried to fly from Chicago to New York City in one day and failed. Still, she set an American nonstop cross-country flying record—590 miles!—and thrilled a nation.

Her record stood for one year. It was broken by Katherine Stinson, another pilot who dared.

THINK AND RESPOND

1 How did Ruth Law thrill the nation?

2 Why do you think the author chose to tell events in sequence?

3 Why do you think the author wanted to tell about Ruth Law's flying **feat**?

4 What do you think it would have been like to be a member of Ruth Law's plane crew?

5 What strategies did you use to read this story?

Visit *The Learning Site!*
www.harcourtschool.com

Meet the Author and Illustrator

Don Brown

Don Brown loves to read and write about history. While writing a magazine article about flight, he became interested in early flyers. He didn't want brave pilots like Ruth Law to be forgotten. This is his first children's book.

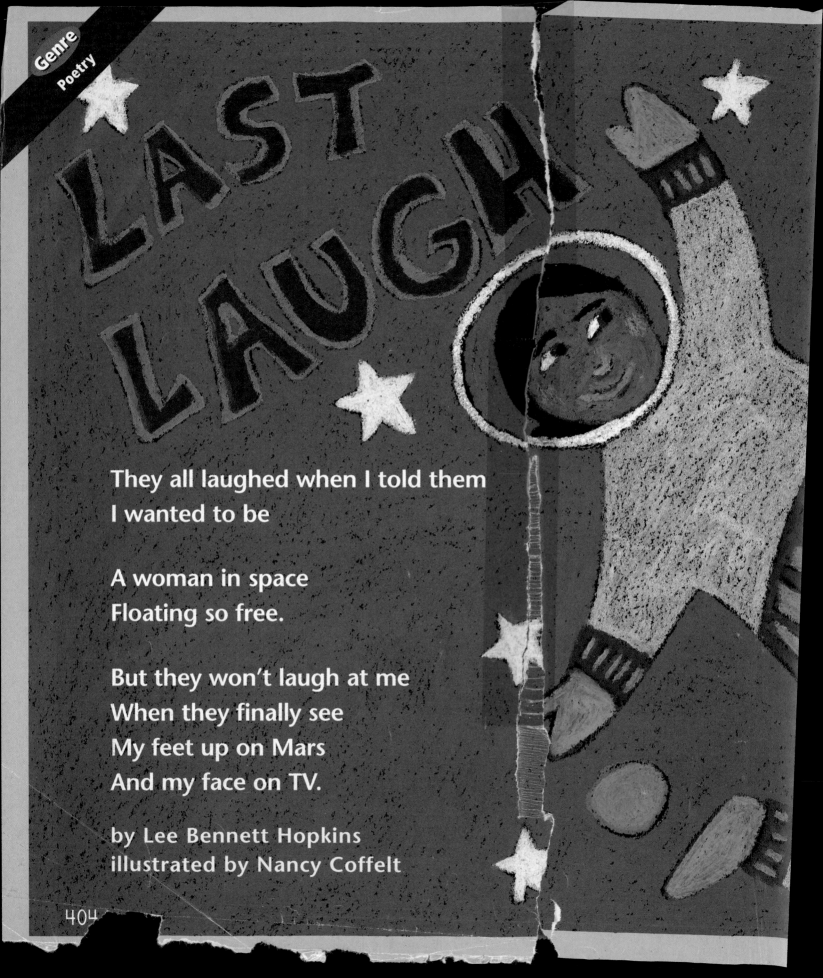

LAST LAUGH

They all laughed when I told them
I wanted to be

A woman in space
Floating so free.

But they won't laugh at me
When they finally see
My feet up on Mars
And my face on TV.

by Lee Bennett Hopkins
illustrated by Nancy Coffelt

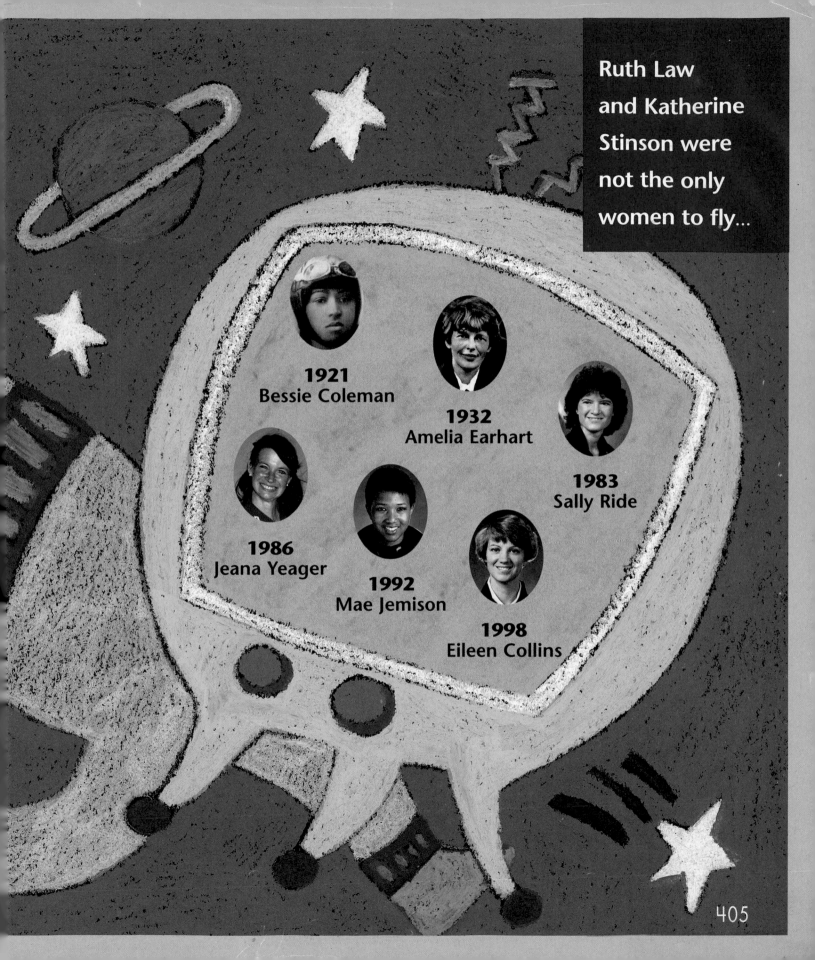

Ruth Law
and Katherine
Stinson were
not the only
women to fly...

1921
Bessie Coleman

1932
Amelia Earhart

1983
Sally Ride

1986
Jeana Yeager

1992
Mae Jemison

1998
Eileen Collins

Making Connections

Compare Texts

1. Why do you think "Ruth Law Thrills a Nation" is part of a theme called Travel Time?

2. How might Don Brown use "Beginner's World Atlas" to give more information about Ruth Law's flight?

3. Think about the narrator of the poem "Last Laugh." How is she like Ruth Law? How is she different?

Journal Entry

November 19, 1916

I am so tired! I have had a long, cold day of flying.

Imagine that you are Ruth Law and have landed in Binghamton for the night. Write a short journal entry about your trip so far. Tell how you feel about flying across the country.

Writing CONNECTION

Airplane Races

Make a paper airplane. Then go outside with your teacher and classmates. Throw your airplane, and use a yardstick or measuring tape to measure how far it goes. With your class, make a chart to compare the distances.

Name	Distance
Emma	37 inches
Duane	42 inches
Ling	55 inches

Map Ruth's Route

Look at a map of the United States. Trace Ruth Law's trip from Chicago to New York City. Which states might she have flown over? Think of two possible routes. Then choose the one you think is better. Share your flight plan with classmates.

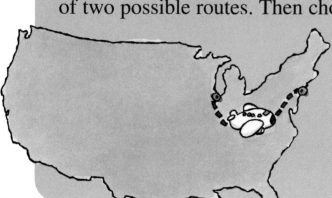

Predict Outcomes

Focus Skill

Story details are like clues in a mystery. You can use them to figure out what will happen next. When you use clues to figure out what will happen, you make a **prediction**.

Look at the chart. Read each clue. Then predict what will happen next.

Clue #1	Clue #2	Prediction
Rosa's friend tells her about the flight museum.	Rosa looks up the address of the flight museum.	*Rosa will go to the flight museum.*
Max's teacher asks him to write a book report.	Max reads a book about Amelia Earhart.	
Ross packs for a trip to his uncle's house.	Ross gets on an airplane.	

Read the story. Then answer the questions.

Nora's Airplane

Nora brought the model airplane kit home from the store. She took the pieces out of the box. Then she read the directions. She carefully glued the pieces together. When the model was finished, she painted it. The airplane gleamed in the light.

1. **Which sentence would go best at the end of the paragraph?**
   - ○ She smiled at her new airplane.
   - ○ She felt sad and angry about the color.
   - ○ She was proud of her model car.

Tip
Read the paragraph with each possible sentence at the end. Choose the sentence that sounds best.

2. **The next thing Nora will do is _____.**
   - ○ throw the airplane away
   - ○ hang the airplane in her room
   - ○ take the airplane apart

Tip
Read all the choices. Choose the one that makes the best sense.

Writer's Handbook

Contents

Planning Your Writing

Purposes for Writing

There are many different **purposes for writing.**
People may write to give information, to entertain, to
give an opinion, or to express ideas.

Some Purposes for Writing	Examples
to give information	• how-to paragraph • research report
to entertain	• funny story • poem
to give an opinion	• poster that persuades • book review
to express ideas	• journal entry • letter

Try This

What would be the purpose for writing a paragraph about
kinds of cats?

The Writing Process

When you write, use a plan to help you. Think about *what* you want to write, for *whom* you are writing, and *why* you are writing. Then use these stages to help you as you write.

Revise
Read what you have written. Add important ideas and details that you left out. Be sure your information is in an order that makes sense.

Draft
Write your ideas in sentences and paragraphs. Do not worry about making mistakes.

Prewrite
Plan what you will write. Choose your topic, and organize your information.

Proofread

Check for errors. Correct mistakes in capital letters, end marks, and spelling.

Publish

Choose a way to share your writing. You can add pictures, graphs, or charts.

Try This

In your journal, list the five writing stages. Draw a picture with five parts like the one above to help you remember each stage.

How to Get Ideas

Writers find **topics,** or ideas, for writing in many ways. One way is to **brainstorm** ideas. When you brainstorm, you make a list of all the ideas that come to your mind. This is a list of ideas for a story about places to play.

Where I Like to Play

backyard

park

my bedroom

Writers also brainstorm ideas by using a **word web.**

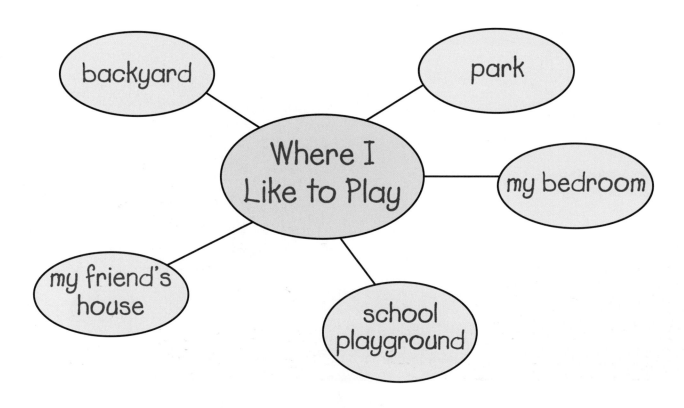

Writers ask **questions** to get ideas for their writing. They write a few questions and then find the answers before they begin writing. These questions are for a research report about trucks.

> Trucks That Help Us
>
> What kinds of trucks help people do jobs?
>
> What do these trucks do?

Another way to get ideas is to write in your **journal.** You can keep a record of interesting things that happen to write about later.

September 2, 2003

Today was my first piano lesson. I was so nervous, but I loved playing! The half hour flew by. My teacher said I did a great job.

Try This

Choose an animal that you would like to write about. Brainstorm a list of words that tell about it.

Dictionary

A **dictionary** is a book that gives the meanings of words. It may also give an example sentence that shows how to use the word. A **synonym,** or word that has the same meaning, may come after the example sentence. The **entry words** are in ABC order, or alphabetical order. If a word has more than one meaning, each meaning has a number.

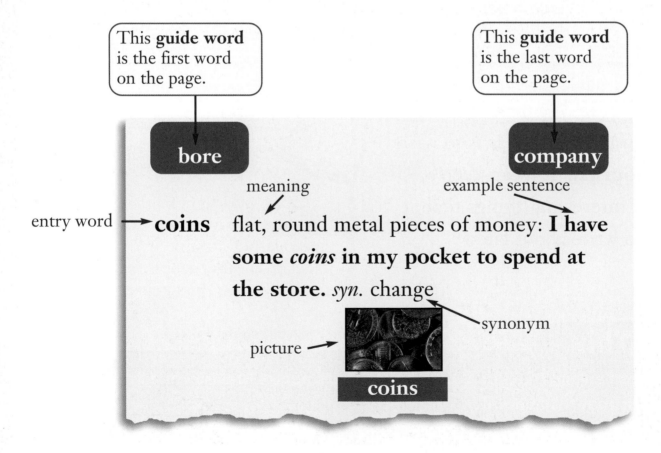

This **guide word** is the first word on the page.

This **guide word** is the last word on the page.

bore

company

meaning

example sentence

entry word → **coins** flat, round metal pieces of money: **I have some** *coins* **in my pocket to spend at the store.** *syn.* change

synonym

picture →

coins

Thesaurus

A **thesaurus** is a list of words and their synonyms. Sometimes a thesaurus lists antonyms, too. An **antonym** is a word that has the opposite meaning. A good time to use a thesaurus is when you are looking for a more interesting word or a more exact word.

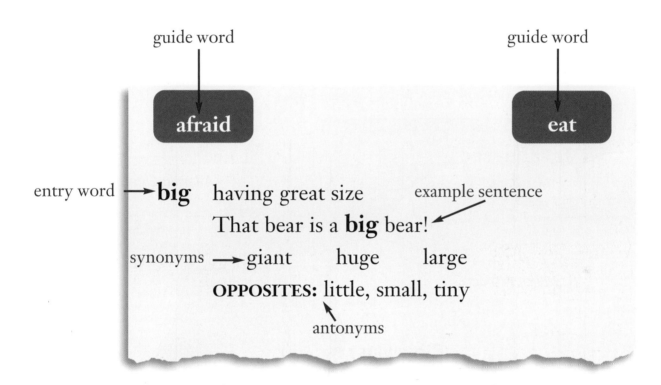

guide word

guide word

afraid

eat

entry word → **big** having great size

That bear is a **big** bear!

example sentence

synonyms → giant   huge   large

OPPOSITES: little, small, tiny

antonyms

Try This

Choose a word. Look it up in the dictionary and in the thesaurus. What do you find that is the same in both books? What is different?

Atlas

An **atlas** is a book of maps. An atlas of the United States has maps of all the states. The maps show cities, bodies of waters, and mountains. Sometimes the maps show where products are made. Look in an atlas's Table of Contents or Index to find the map you need.

Map of Florida

Newspaper

A **newspaper** gives the news. It can tell what is happening around the world and in your town.

A newspaper tells about many subjects. It can tell about neighborhood events, sports, art, business, and the weather. Newspaper articles tell *who, what, where, when, why,* and *how.*

Magazine

A **magazine** gives information in stories and pictures. Magazines usually come out once a week or once a month.

Magazines can be about one main subject, such as science, skating, baseball, or doll collecting. Some magazines are written for certain groups of people, such as children, parents, or older people.

Try This

Find a newspaper article about a place. Find the place in an atlas. What does the atlas tell about it?

Parts of a Book

Most books have special pages that give information about what is inside. The **table of contents,** in the front, shows the chapters of a book. It also gives the page number for the beginning of each chapter.

A **glossary,** at the back, tells the meanings of important words in the book.

Table of Contents

An **index,** also at the back, lists the subjects in the book. The subjects are in alphabetical order. The index gives the page numbers where you can find those subjects.

Index

Using a Computer

A computer can help you in many ways as you write. You can use **spell-check** to find and correct words that are misspelled.

You can use a computer's **search engine** to find information. A **key word** tells what your topic is. Type a key word and click on *Go*.

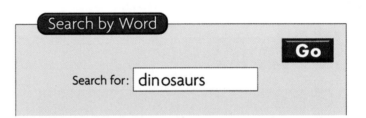

You can also use a computer to get and send e-mail messages. To send e-mail, you need a person's e-mail address.

Try This

Find a book about your favorite sport. Look at the table of contents. Choose a chapter that interests you and read some of it. Then use a word-processing program to write a short paragraph about what you read.

Story

A story has a beginning, a middle, and an end. A good story has strong characters, a setting, and a problem to solve.

A **story map** is a chart that shows the parts of a story. Writers use story maps to plan their stories during the prewriting stage. A writer answers the questions in each part of the story map.

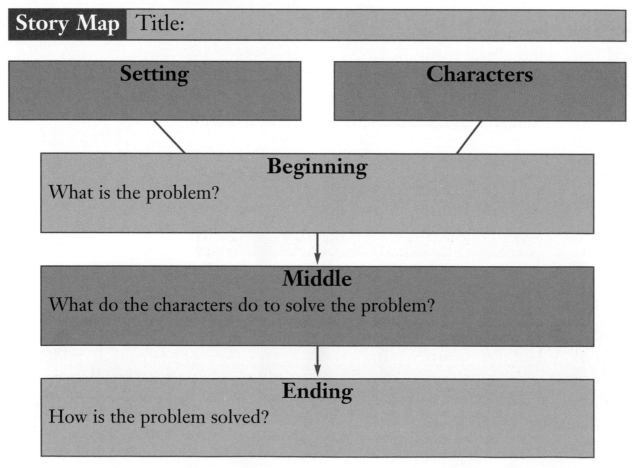

Story Map	Title:

Setting

Characters

Beginning
What is the problem?

Middle
What do the characters do to solve the problem?

Ending
How is the problem solved?

A **sequence chart** is another way to organize a story. Writers often use sequence charts to write personal stories. In a **personal story,** a writer tells about something that happened in his or her life.

In a sequence chart, the writer answers questions about what happens **first, next,** and **last** in a personal story.

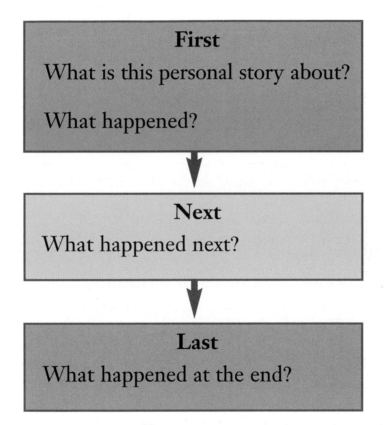

First

What is this personal story about?

What happened?

Next

What happened next?

Last

What happened at the end?

Try This

Think about a story you know. Make a story map to show the parts of the story.

Report: Note Taking

In a **research report,** a writer gives information about a topic. To find information for a report, you can write questions on **note cards.** Then search on a computer and at the library to find the answers. Write the answers on your note cards.

> ### When did dinosaurs live?
>
> - The last dinosaur died about 65 million years ago.
> - The first dinosaur lived about 245 million years ago.
> - No one knows for sure why they died.

Put your note cards in an order that makes sense. Then use the cards to write an outline. An **outline** shows the order of **main ideas** and **details** in a piece of writing.

> ### Dinosaurs Outline
>
> 1. When did Dinosaurs live?
>   a. last dinosaur, 65 million years ago
>   b. first dinosaur, 245 million years ago
>   c. No one knows why they died.
> 2. What kinds of dinosaurs were there?
>   a. Tyrannosaurus rex
>   b. Stegosaurus
>   c. Troodon

Use your outline to organize your report. The questions become the **main ideas.** Write a paragraph about each main idea. The answers you found are the **details** about the main ideas.

Dinosaurs

Dinosaurs lived millions of years ago. The first dinosaurs lived about 245 million years ago. The last dinosaurs died about 65 million years ago. No one is sure why this happened.

Many different kinds of dinosaurs roamed the Earth. Tyrannosaurus rex was big and fierce and weighed more than 1,400 pounds. Stegosaurus had bony plates on its back. Troodon weighed less than 100 pounds, but some scientists think it was one of the smartest dinosaurs.

Try This

Think about what you do on a weekend morning. Take notes about what you do, and write an outline.

Traits of Good Writing

All good writers ask themselves questions like these about what they write.

Focus/Ideas

- Is my message clear and interesting?
- Do I have enough information?

Organization

- Do I have a good beginning and a good ending?
- Is my information or my story in the right order?

Development

- Do each of my paragraphs have a main idea?
- Do I include important details in my paragraphs?

Voice

- Do I sound like myself?
- Do I say in an interesting way what I think or feel?

Word Choice

- Do my words make sense?
- Do I use interesting words?

Sentences

- Do I begin my sentences in different ways?
- Does my writing sound smooth when I read it aloud?

Conventions

- Do I indent my paragraphs?
- Are my spelling, punctuation marks, and capital letters correct?

Writers use **editor's marks** like these as they **revise** and **proofread** their writing.

Editor's Marks

⌃	Change.
℮	Take out.
≡	Use a capital letter.
⌃,	Add a comma.
⌄⁓	Add quotation marks.

Try This

Read a story with a partner. Talk about the traits of good writing that you find in the story.

Using a Rubric

A **rubric** is a checklist you can use to make your writing better. Here is how you can use a rubric.

Before writing   Look at the checklist to find out what your piece of writing should have.

During writing   Check your draft against the list. Use the list to see how to make your writing better.

After writing   Check your finished work against the list. Does your work show all the points?

Your Best Score

✔ Your writing is focused.

✔ You write about your ideas in an order that makes sense.

✔ You give important details about the main idea.

✔ Your writing sounds like you.

✔ You use words that are clear.

✔ Your sentences begin differently and fit together well.

✔ Your writing has few or no mistakes in punctuation, capitalization, or grammar.

Peer Conferences

After you have written your first draft, you are ready to revise your writing. A class partner can help. Follow these steps to have a peer conference. A **peer conference** is a meeting with a partner or small group to help you make your writing better.

Revising Your Writing

1. Read your first draft aloud. Then let your partner read it silently.

2. Talk with your partner about ways to make your draft better.

3. Take notes about changes you need to make.

Revising Your Partner's Writing

1. Listen carefully to your partner's draft read aloud. Then read it slowly yourself.

2. Tell two or three things that you like about it.

3. Give your partner one or two suggestions for making the draft better.

Try This

Meet with a partner to talk about your writing. Together, go over the traits of good writing. Talk about the traits your writing has.

Handwriting Tips

It is important to write neatly and clearly so that others can read your writing. Follow these handwriting tips.

- Hold your pencil and place your paper as shown.

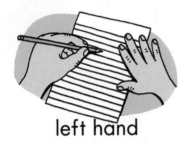
left hand

right hand

- Sit up straight. Face your desk, and place both feet on the floor.

- Make your letters smooth and even.

- Make sure your letters are not too close together or too far apart.

correct	too close	too far apart
great	great	g r e a t

- Begin writing to the right of the red line on your paper. Leave a space as wide as a pencil.

- The space between words or between sentences should be as wide as a pencil.

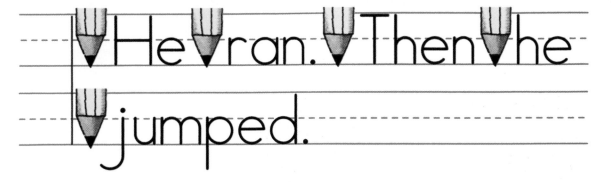

- Make sure tall letters touch the top line, short letters touch the midline, and the tails of letters hang below the base line.

Try This

Use your best handwriting to write a letter to a friend.

Using Computer Graphics

You can use your computer to add graphics, or pieces of art, to your writing.

- **Use different kinds of type.** Using different kinds of type and different colors makes writing fun to read.

- **Add pictures to a story.** Use pictures from your word processing program, or use a separate drawing program. Add art to your story to make a book.

- **Add frames and borders.**

- **Add charts or graphs to a report.** Use your computer to make charts and graphs. Show them as you share your report with your classmates.

Pictograph

Books Read in October				
Tom	📖	📖	📖	📖
Ann	📖	📖	📖	
Sam	📖	📖	📖	📖	📖
Beth	📖	📖	📖	📖
Key: 📖 = 1 book				

Bar Graph

Books Read in October					
Tom					
Ann					
Sam					
Beth					
	1	2	3	4	5

Oral Presentations

You may want to give an **oral presentation** of your writing. Here are some ways to keep your listeners interested.

- Plan your presentation. Decide how you will read or present your writing.

- Hold your paper low so that listeners can see your face.

- Look at your listeners when you speak.

- Use your voice to show funny, sad, or exciting parts of your writing.

- Speak loudly and clearly so that everyone can hear you.

- Use drawings, charts, or time lines to help make your writing interesting and clear.

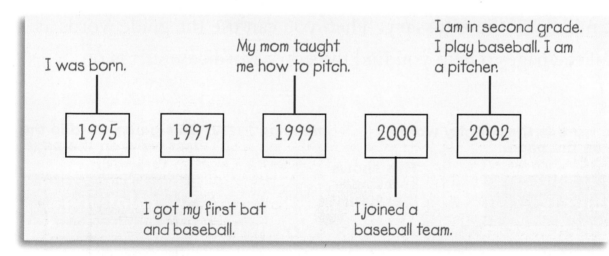

I was born. 1995

I got my first bat and baseball. 1997

My mom taught me how to pitch. 1999

I joined a baseball team. 2000

I am in second grade. I play baseball. I am a pitcher. 2002

Try This

Think about something exciting that happened to you. Tell three things you would do to make listeners feel that it is exciting.

Using the Glossary

Get to Know It!

The **Glossary** gives the meaning of a word as it is used in the story. It also gives an example sentence that shows how to use the word. A **synonym**, which is a word that has the same meaning, a **base word**, or **additional word forms** may come after the example sentence. The words in the **Glossary** are in ABC order, also called **alphabetical order**.

Learn to Use It!

If you want to find *oceans* in the **Glossary**, you should first find the *O* words. *O* is near the middle of the alphabet, so the *O* words are near the middle of the **Glossary**. Then you can use the guide words at the top of the page to help you find the entry word *oceans*. It is on page 441.

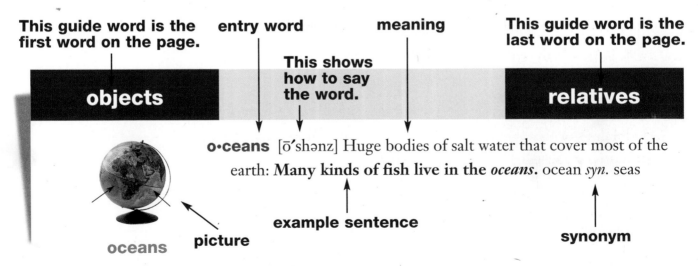

This guide word is the first word on the page.

entry word

meaning

This guide word is the last word on the page.

This shows how to say the word.

objects

relatives

o·ceans [ō′shənz] Huge bodies of salt water that cover most of the earth: **Many kinds of fish live in the *oceans*.** ocean *syn.* seas

oceans

picture

example sentence

synonym

A

ad·dress·es [ə·dres′əz] The information on pieces of mail telling whom the mail is for and where those people live: **Make sure the *addresses* on the envelopes are correct so the people will get the letters.** address

ad·mired [ad·mīrd′] Liked something or someone: **Sarah's classmates *admired* the nice card she had made.** admire, admiring

ap·peared [ə·pird′] Came into sight: **The rabbit ran into a hole, but it *appeared* again a few minutes later.** appear, appearing

addresses

B

bor·ing [bôr′ing] Not interesting: **Some stories are exciting, but that story is *boring*.**

C

cap·tured [kap′chərd] Caught and held by someone: **The horse that ran away was *captured* and brought back to the barn.** capture, capturing

cas·sette [kə·set′] A case holding a spool of tape for putting into a tape recorder or player: **We listened to my favorite *cassette* tape.**

caused [kôzd] Made something happen: **He jumped up so fast that he *caused* the chair to fall over.** cause, causing

cel·e·bra·tions [sel·ə·brā′shənz] Parties or festivals held to mark special days or to honor people: **Our family has many birthday *celebrations* each year.** celebrate, celebration

435

clasp

clerk

conductor

dappled

clasp [klasp] A small piece that holds the ends of something together: **She opened the *clasp* on her necklace and took the necklace off.**

clerk [klûrk] A person who sells things in a store: **The *clerk* at the market took my money and gave me my change.**

com·pan·ions [kəm•pan′yənz] People who spend time together: **My *companions* and I play in the park every day.** companion

con·duc·tor [kən•duk′tər] The person who helps the people riding on a train: **The *conductor* called out each stop so people would know when to get off the train.**

con·fused [kən•fyo͞ozd′] Mixed up; not sure of what is happening: **Jim felt *confused* by all the traffic and noise in the big city.**

connects [kə•nekts′] Joins: **This road *connects* our street to the highway.** connect

cor·nered [kôr′nərd] Trapped, as if in a corner from which one cannot escape: **It looked as if the dog had the cat *cornered*, but it got away.**

co·zy [kō′zē] Warm and comfortable: **We put a blanket in the puppy's basket to make it *cozy* for him.** *syn.* snug

cre·at·ed [krē•āt′əd] Used skill or art to make something new: **The children *created* many pictures and stories.** create, creating

dap·pled [dap′əld] Having spots or patches of a different color: **The *dappled* fawns will lose their white spots when they grow up.**

de·tails [di•tālz′ or dē′tālz] Facts about something: **Tell me the *details* of your trip.** detail

de·vel·op [di•vel′əp] To come or bring to full growth: **With enough water and sunlight, these tiny plants will *develop* into huge trees.** develops, developing

dis·ap·point [dis•ə•point′] To make someone feel bad by not doing what they want you to do: **I know it will *disappoint* my friend if I don't go to her party.** disappointed, disappointing

dis·tance [dis′təns] The space between two points: **Can you measure the *distance* the football traveled?**

drift·ed [drift′əd] Was carried along by water or air: **When Kim let go of the kite string, her kite *drifted* away.** drift, drifting

ducked [dukt] Got down quickly to keep from being hit by something: **When Jody saw the ball coming, he *ducked* so he wouldn't be hit.** duck, ducking

ducked

E

ex·hi·bi·tion [ek•sə•bish′ən] A display that people come to see: **The museum is having an *exhibition* of paintings by children.**

F

feat [fēt] Something that takes a lot of skill and courage: **Climbing the highest mountain in the world is a great *feat*.**

fea·tures [fē′chərz] The most important parts of something: **One of the nicest *features* of the park is the picnic area.** feature

fleet [flēt] A group of ships or boats that sail together: **We saw a *fleet* of sailboats heading out to sea.**

fleet

flip·pers [flip′ərz] Wide, flat legs that help water animals swim: **The seals clapped their *flippers* at the marine park.** flipper

437

glide

harbor

flock [flok] A group of animals or birds that eat or travel together: **A** *flock* **of about 100 sheep ate grass on the hill.**

for•ci•bly [fôr′sə•blē] Done in a strong way: **The puppy would not come out of the doghouse and had to be** *forcibly* **removed.**

fu•ri•ous [fyŏŏr′ē•əs] Very angry: **My father was** *furious* **with me when I disobeyed him.**

fussed [fust] Acted upset about something: **The little children** *fussed* **as they waited in the long line.** fuss, fussing

glide [glīd] To move in a smooth way: **Watch the eagle** *glide* **across the sky.** glided, gliding

grace•ful [grās′fəl] Able to move in a smooth and beautiful way: **Dancers are** *graceful* **both on and off the stage.**

gro•cer•y store [grō′sər•ē stôr] A place where food and household goods are sold: **Besides foods, our new** *grocery store* **sells school supplies, dishes, and even fresh flowers.**

grown [grōn] Finished growing: **That cute little puppy has** *grown* **to become a big dog.** grow, grew, growing

har•bor [här′bər] A place where ships can anchor or be protected in a storm. **The ship sailed into the** *harbor* **after its long trip across the ocean.**

hatch [hach] To come out of an egg: **The baby chicks are beginning to** *hatch.*

haze [hāz] Misty or dusty air, such as you might see on a very hot day: **We could not see the tops of the tall buildings through the** *haze*.

her·o·ine [her′ō·in] A woman or girl who has done something brave or special; a woman or girl who is a hero: **Everyone called Molly a** *heroine* **after she saved the kitten from the pond.**

hon·or [on′ər] A show of pride in someone or something: **We fly the flag in** *honor* **of our country.**

ho·ri·zon [hə·rī′zən] The line where the earth seems to meet the sky: **We were already awake when the sun rose over the** *horizon*.

horizon

hos·pi·tal·i·ty [hos·pə·tal′ə·tē] A nice way of treating guests: **We like to eat there because the** *hospitality* **is as good as the food.**

I

im·ag·i·na·tion [i·maj·ə·nā′shən] The thoughts people use to pretend or to make up stories: **The author must have had a great** *imagination* **to write a story about talking rocks.**

im·i·tat·ed [im′ə·tāt·əd] Copied the way something looked, acted, or sounded: **Jenny** *imitated* **the dance steps she saw on television.** imitate, imitating

imitated

in·for·ma·tion [in·fər·mā′shən] Facts: **We went to the library for** *information* **about frogs.**

L

land·scape busi·ness [land′skāp biz′nis] A kind of business in which workers make outdoor places look better by adding plants and changing the land: **Workers in a** *landscape business* **need to know a lot about flowers, trees, and other plants.**

439

launched [lôncht] Moved, like a boat, from land into the water: **The people on the dock cheered when the ship was *launched* into the sea.**

loom·ing [lo͞om′ing] Coming into sight looking large and scary: **We saw the old house *looming* before us on the dark hill.** loom, loomed

lug·gage [lug′ij] Suitcases and bags used in traveling: **We put our *luggage* in the car.**

man·ners [man′ərz] Ways of acting that show that a person is polite: **Children who have good *manners* do not play with their food.**

map·mak·er [map′māk•ər] A person who makes a drawing that shows where things are located: **I would love to watch a *mapmaker* draw a map of my town.**

mat·a·dor [mat′ə•dôr] A person who fights bulls for sport: **The *matador* waved his red cape as the bull ran around the ring.**

mim·icked [mim′ikt] Copied what someone else said or did: **The boys bent their knees and *mimicked* the funny way the circus clown walked.** mimic, mimicking

mis·er·a·ble [miz′ər•ə•bəl] Very unhappy: **Jay was *miserable* when he was sick with the flu.**

no·tice [nō′tis] To see or pay attention to: **We didn't *notice* the dark clouds in the sky until it began to rain.** noticed, noticing

ob·jects [ob′jikts] Things that can be seen or touched: **The bag was filled with small *objects*, such as coins, buttons, and toys.** object

o·ceans [ō′shənz] Huge bodies of salt water that cover most of the earth: **Many kinds of fish live in the *oceans*.** ocean *syn.* seas

pale [pāl] Light in color: **I mixed white paint and green paint to make a *pale* green color.**

peel [pēl] To strip away or remove: **Bananas are the easiest kind of fruit to *peel*.**

plains [plānz] Flat lands with no trees: **The open *plains* stretched ahead of us as far as we could see.**

pour [pôr] To move in a steady stream: **Children pour out the school's front door when the bell rings.** poured, pouring

ranch [ranch] A kind of large farm where cows, horses, or sheep are raised: **It took the cowhands all day to move the cattle from one part of the *ranch* to another.**

re·al·ized [rē′əl·īzd] Came to understand something: **After a few tries, the boys *realized* that they needed a longer rope.** realize, realizing

re·fused [ri·fyōozd′] Did not do what was asked: **Mother *refused* to give us ice cream before dinner.** refuse, refusing

rel·a·tives [rel′ə·tivz] People in the same family: **My aunts, uncles, cousins, and other *relatives* came to the party.** relative

oceans

plains

ranch

relax

spectators

stroke

re·lax [ri•laks'] Take a rest: **After playing ball, we like to sit down and *relax*.** relaxed, relaxing

re·moves [ri•mōōvz'] Takes something off: **He *removes* his shoes and puts on his slippers.** remove, removed, removing

rhythm [rith'əm] A set of sounds repeated again and again: **We clapped our hands to the *rhythm* of the music.**

route [rōōt or rout] The path that a salesperson or delivery person follows: **Our newspaper carrier follows her *route* every day.**

sense [sens] A correct way of thinking: **It makes *sense* to wear a helmet when you ride a bike.**

slip·per·y [slip'ər•ē] Slick and hard to hold onto or stand on: **The sidewalk is very *slippery* when it is covered with ice.**

soared [sôrd] Flew high into the air: **The bird *soared* high above the earth on its strong wings.** soar, soaring

spec·ta·tors [spek'tā•tərz] People who watch something: **The *spectators* cheered when the batter hit a home run.** spectator

star·tled [stär'təld] Surprised and frightened: **The sudden noise *startled* me and made me drop my cup.** startle, startling

stood [stŏŏd] Stayed the same: **The record for the most home runs *stood* for many years.** stand, standing

stroke [strōk] Rub in a gentle way: **My cat likes it when I *stroke* her back.** stroked, stroking

stu·dents [stŏŏd'ənts] People who learn in a school: **The *students* in Mrs. Santiago's second-grade class are learning Spanish.** *syn.* pupil

stur·dy [stûr'dē] Strong: **The little tree grew to be tall and *sturdy*.**

sup·pose [sə•pōz´] To think something is likely: **Dad's car is in the driveway, so I *suppose* he must be home.** supposed, supposing

swoop·ing [swōōp´ing] Coming down in a wide, curving movement: **The hawk was *swooping* down from the sky.** swoop, swooped

thou·sands [thou´zəndz] Many, many hundreds: **There are *thousands* of leaves on that big oak tree.** thousand

trac·tor [trak´tər] A machine used for pulling a plow: **Kim loves to watch her uncle plow with his *tractor* at the farm.**

typ·i·cal [tip´i•kəl] Very much like other things of the same kind: **A *typical* school day includes reading and math lessons.**

va·ca·tion [vā•kā´shən] Time off from school or work: **When summer *vacation* is over, it's time to go back to school.**

wad·dled [wod´əld] Swayed from side to side when walking: **The duck *waddled* to the pond.** waddle, waddling

Index *of* Titles

Page numbers in color tell where you can read about the author.

Acknowledgments

For permission to reprint copyrighted material, grateful acknowledgment is made to the following sources:

Curtis Brown, Ltd.: "Last Laugh" from *Blast Off! Poems About Space* by Lee Bennett Hopkins. Text copyright © 1974 by Lee Bennett Hopkins. Published by HarperCollins Publishers.

Candlewick Press Inc., Cambridge, MA, on behalf of Walker Books Ltd., London: *The Emperor's Egg* by Martin Jenkins, illustrated by Jane Chapman. Text © 1999 by Martin Jenkins; illustrations © 1999 by Jane Chapman.

Children's Better Health Institute, Indianapolis, IN: "Keeping a Road Journal" by Joy Beck, illustrated by Patti H. Goodnow from *Jack and Jill* Magazine. Copyright © 1996 by Children's Better Health Institute, Benjamin Franklin Literary & Medical Society, Inc.

Children's Television Workshop, New York, NY: "Cool It!" by Lynn O'Donnell from *3-2-1 Contact* Magazine, July/August 1997. Text copyright 1997 by Children's Television Workshop. From "Birds Do It! Recycle!" in *Kid City* Magazine, April 1995. Text copyright 1995 by Children's Television Workshop.

Clarion Books/Houghton Mifflin Company: *Anthony Reynoso: Born to Rope* by Martha Cooper and Ginger Gordon. Text copyright © 1996 by Ginger Gordon; photographs copyright © 1996 by Martha Cooper.

Crown Publishers, Inc.: *How I Spent My Summer Vacation* by Mark Teague. Copyright © 1995 by Mark Teague.

Dial Books for Young Readers, a division of Penguin Putnam Inc.: From *Snakey Riddles* by Katy Hall and Lisa Eisenberg, illustrated by Simms Taback. Text copyright © 1990 by Katy Hall and Lisa Eisenberg; illustrations copyright © 1990 by Simms Taback. *The Day Jimmy's Boa Ate the Wash* by Trinka Hakes Noble, illustrated by Steven Kellogg. Text copyright © 1980 by Trinka Hakes Noble; illustrations copyright © 1980 by Steven Kellogg.

Dutton Children's Books, a division of Penguin Putnam Inc.: *Abuela* by Arthur Dorros, illustrated by Elisa Kleven. Text copyright © 1991 by Arthur Dorros; illustrations copyright © 1991 by Elisa Kleven.

HarperCollins Publishers: *Good-bye, Curtis* by Kevin Henkes, illustrated by Marisabina Russo. Text copyright © 1995 by Kevin Henkes; illustrations copyright © 1995 by Marisabina Russo.

David Higham Associates: "City Music" by Tony Mitton from *Poems Go Clang!* Text © 1997 by Tony Mitton. Published by Candlewick Press.

Holiday House, Inc.: "June" from *A Child's Calendar* by John Updike, illustrated by Trina Schart Hyman. Text copyright © 1965, 1999 by John Updike; illustrations copyright © 1999 by Trina Schart Hyman.

Henry Holt and Company, LLC: *Chinatown* by William Low. Copyright © 1997 by William Low.

Little, Brown and Company (Inc.): From *Dinosaurs Travel* by Laurie Krasny Brown and Marc Brown. Copyright © 1988 by Laurie Krasny Brown and Marc Brown.

Margaret K. McElderry Books, an imprint of Simon & Schuster Children's Publishing Division: *Dear Mr. Blueberry* by Simon James. Copyright © 1991 by Simon James. Originally published in Great Britain by Walker Books, Ltd. *Cool Ali* by Nancy Poydar. Copyright © 1996 by Nancy Poydar.

National Geographic Society: From *National Geographic Beginner's World Atlas*. Copyright © 1999 by National Geographic Society.

Simon & Schuster Books for Young Readers, an imprint of Simon & Schuster Children's Publishing Division: *Max Found Two Sticks* by Brian Pinkney. Copyright © 1994 by Brian Pinkney.

Ticknor & Fields Books for Young Readers/Houghton Mifflin Company: *Ruth Law Thrills a Nation* by Don Brown. Copyright © 1993 by Don Brown.

Viking Penguin, a division of Penguin Putnam Inc.: *Montigue On the High Seas* by John Himmelman. Copyright © 1988 by John Himmelman.

Franklin Watts, a Division of Grolier Publishing: From "Sports and Exercise" in *Look What Came From China* by Miles Harvey. Text © 1998 by Franklin Watts, a Division of Grolier Publishing.

Photo Credits

Key: (t) = top; (b) = bottom; (c) = center; (l) = left; (r) = right.
Page 32, courtesy, Penguin Putman; 33, Tom Sobolik / Black Star; 40(t), Werner Bertsch / Bruce Coleman, Inc.; 40(b), Dennis Degnan / Corbis; 41(t), Ernest Janes / Bruce Coleman, Inc.; 41(b), Superstock; 59, Black Star; 89, courtesy, Walker Books; 113, Rick Friedman / Black Star; 115(t), G.C. Kelly / Photo Researchers, Inc.; 115(c), Jim Cummins / FPG; 115(b), Jeffrey Sylverster / FPG; 116(t), Rod Planck / Photo Researchers, Inc.; 116(c), Anthony Merceca / Photo Researchers, Inc.; 116(b), John Cancalosi / Tom Stack & Associates; 117(t), John Gerlach / Tom Stack & Associates; 117(c), Renee Lynn / Photo Researchers, Inc.; 122(t), Mark A. Chappell / Animals Animals; 122(b), Keith Kent / SPL / Photo Researchers, Inc.; 123(t), Superstock; 123(b), Richard Kolar / Animals Animals; 145(l), David Levenson / Black Star; 145(r), courtesy, Walker Books; 169(l), Black Star; 169(r), Mark Derse; 170, Roger Wilmshurst / Bruce Coleman, Inc.; 176(t), Michele Burgess / Corbis Stock Market; 176(b), Spencer Grant / Photo Researchers, Inc.; 177(t), Amy Dunleavy; 177(b), Mug Shots / Corbis Stock Market; 194, Black Star; 195, 221, Tom Sobolik / Black Star; 230-245, Martha Cooper; 250(t), Gail Mooney / Corbis; 250(b), Robbie Jack / Corbis; 251(t), Stone; 251(b), Robert Young Pelton / Corbis; 271, Erich Lansner / Black Star; 272, Ann Chwatsky; 273(t), C. Ursillo / H. Armstrong Roberts; 273(b), H. Armstrong Roberts; 280(t), Superstock; 280(b), Rod Planck / Dembinsky Photo Associates; 281(t), Alese & MortPechter / Corbis Stock Market; 281(b), Sam Fried / Photo Researchers, Inc.; 300, Black Star; 301, Dale Higgins; 306, Keith Gunnar / Bruce Coleman, Inc.; 308(tl), Paul Chesley / Stone; 308(tr), Michael Scott / Stone; 308(bl), Ed Simpson / Stone; 308(bc), Connie Coleman / Stone; 308(br), Nicholas DeVore / Stone; 309(t), T. Davis, W. Bilenduke / Stone; 309(b), Frans Lanting / Stone; 314, NASA; 320(2nd), Hugh Sitton / Stone; 320(3rd), Steven Weinberg / Stone; 320(b), Cosmo Condina / Stone; 321(t), Michael Nichols / National Geographic Society; 321(2nd), Andrea Booher / Stone; 321(3rd), Greg Probst / Stone; 321(4th), Stephen & Michele Vaughan; 321(b), Tom Bean; 322, Ed Simpson / Stone; 323, Rosemary Calvert / Stone; 326(tr), Charles Krebs / Stone; 326(cl), Mark Lewis / Stone; 326(b), Bruce Wilson / Stone; 327(t), Dave Bartruff / Artistry International; 327(c), Stephen Krasemann / Stone; 327(b), Stone; 330(tr), Gary Brettnacher / Stone; 330(cl), Mark Lewis / Stone; 330(cr), Ncik Gunderson / Stone; 330(cb), Cosmo Condina / Stone; 330(bl), David Hiser / Stone; 331(tl), George Hunter / Stone; 331(cr), Will & Deni McIntyre / Stone; 336(t), Rob Lewine / Corbis Stock Market; 336(b), McCarthy / Corbis Stock Market; 337(t), Myrleen Ferguson / PhotoEdit; 337(b), Superstock; 356, 357, Rick Friedman / Black Star; 379, Black Star; 405(tl), The Granger Collection, New York; 405(tc), Culver Pictures; 405(tr), NASA; 405(bl), Liaison Agency; 405(bc), NASA; 405(br), NASA / Photo Researchers, Inc.; 416, 434, Harcourt Photo Library; 435, Ken Kinzie / Harcourt; 436(t), Victoria Bowen / Harcourt; 436(2nd), Harcourt Photo Library; 436(3rd), Kindra Clineff / Index Stock; 436(b), Stephen J. Krasemann / Photo Researchers, Inc.; 438(t), Daniel J. Cox / Stone; 438(b), Jose Funte Raga / Corbis Stock Market; 439, Herb Schmitz / Stone; 441(t), Harcourt Photo Library; 441(c), Ken Martin / Visuals Unlimited; 441(b), D. R. Stoecklein / Corbis Stock Market; 442(t), Charles Krebs / Corbis Stock Market; 442(b), Claude Charlier / Corbis Stock Market.

Illustration Credits

Steve Johnson/Lou Fancher, Cover Art; Gary Taxali, 4-5, 12-13; Will Terry, 6-7, 150-151; Jennifer Beck-Harris, 8-9, 278-279; Ethan Long 10-11, 36-37, 408; Clare Schaumann, 14-15; Steven Kellogg, 16-33; Simms Taback, 34-35; Mark Teague, 42-59; Nancy Davis, 62-63, 225, 226, 382; Donna Perrone, 66-67; Simon James, 68-89; Jackie Snider, 92-93, 247, 173; Kathi Ember, 96-97; Nancy Poydar, 98-113; Tuko Fujisaki, 119, 303, 406-407; Nancy Coffelt, 120, 147, 275, 333, 404-405; Jane Chapman, 124-145; Cathy Bennett, 148, 197; Ande Cook, 152-153; Mary GrandPré, 154-169; Marisabina Russo, 178-195; Geneviéve Després, 200-201; Brian Pinkney, 202-221; Liz Conrad, 222-223; Craig Spearing, 228-229; William Low, 252-271; Mou-sien Tseng, 272-273; Elisa Kleven, 282-301; Marc Brown, 338-357; Liz Callen, 358-359; Laura Ovresat, 360-361; Amanda Harvey, 364-365; John Himmelman, 366-379; Chris Van Dusen, 380-381; Gail Piazza, 384-385; Don Brown, 386-403; Holly Cooper, 437, 440, 442.